Penguin Critic

Gulliver's Travels

Clive Probyn is Professor of English at Monash University, Victoria, Australia. After graduating from Nottingham and Virginia universities he taught for ten years at the University of Lancaster, then became Foundation Professor of English and Dean of Arts at the University of Sokoto, Nigeria, from 1978 to 1980. He has published many articles on eighteenth-century English literature; his editorial work includes the Everyman *Gulliver's Travels* and the *Collected Poems* of Pope. His previous books on Swift are (as editor and contributor) *The Art of Jonathan Swift* and *Jonathan Swift: The Contemporary Background* (1978). *English Poetry: A Handbook* appeared in 1984 and *English Fiction: 1700–1789* is forthcoming. He is currently writing an eighteenth-century biography for Oxford University Press.

Penguin Critical Studies

Joint Advisory Editors:
Stephen Coote and Bryan Loughrey

Jonathan Swift

Gulliver's Travels

Clive T. Probyn

Penguin Books

PENGUIN BOOKS

Published by the Penguin Group
27 Wrights Lane, London W8 5TZ, England
Viking Penguin Inc., 40 West 23rd Street, New York, New York 10010, USA
Penguin Books Australia Ltd, Ringwood, Victoria, Australia
Penguin Books Canada Ltd, 2801 John Street, Markham, Ontario, Canada L3R 1B4
Penguin Books (NZ) Ltd, 182–190 Wairau Road, Auckland 10, New Zealand

Penguin Books Ltd, Registered Offices: Harmondsworth, Middlesex, England

First published as a Penguin Masterstudy 1987
Reprinted as a Penguin Critical Study 1989
10 9 8 7 6 5 4 3 2 1

Made and printed in Great Britain by
Richard Clay Ltd, Bungay, Suffolk
Filmset in Monophoto Times

For David Woolley
amicus et Swiftiani hospes

Contents

Preface

This is primarily a book about *Gulliver's Travels*, Swift's complex master-piece which always has and always will defeat the reader who looks to it for final solutions to the paradox of human nature. I have approached the *Travels* by a direct route in chapter 3, but in the Introduction and in subsequent chapters I draw on a wider range of Swift's writings: *A Tale of a Tub*, some of his poetry, *A Modest Proposal*, his correspondence, and short prose works such as *The Drapier's Letters*. The *Travels* was only one part of a lifetime devoted to several genres – poetry, religious, economic and political tracts, sermons, history, the informal letter. It is a work in which almost everything else Swift wrote about is reflected, and in which Swift could see mirrored the experiences of his own career before 1726.

Swift's satirical eye was also fixed upon the reader. One com-mentator has observed that 'the world of print was made to order for Swift: it offers him personal anonymity, self-concealment ... How much confidence does he inspire in us that we have read him as he meant?' To some extent what Swift *means* is separable from the method of his saying it: it is not very difficult to find 'serious' state-ments which allow us to disentangle Swift's 'ironic' statements on politics, religion, his view of man, and literature itself. But the source of Swift's permanent fascination does not lie in the truth or factuality of his writing. It lies in a kind of perception for which irony, a tech-nique of double meaning, is the only vehicle. Swift's irony is the means by which contraries are maintained, not united, and the simplifications of satire are designed to show up some of the deepest contradictions in civilized society. Although Swift absorbed from his own society its specific preoccupations and historical circumstances, and consequently requires his modern reader to know something about the materials upon which his mind worked, there is a permanent value attached to Swift's sceptical, powerfully analytical satire which attracts more read-ers now than in his own day. What the King of Brobdingnag sees in Gulliver's account of seventeenth-century European history, 'only an Heap of Conspiracies, Rebellions, Murders, Massacres, Revolutions, Banishments', is the stuff of newspaper headlines in the twentieth cen-tury. Swift's satires may not show us the way out of the human dilemma, but they do show us the processes we adopt to fool ourselves that we have no part to play in its perpetration.

Note on Texts, and Abbreviations

The standard text of *Gulliver's Travels* used here is that established by
Herbert Davis for volume XI of his *Prose Writings of Jonathan Swift*, 16
volumes, Oxford, 1941, reprinted in 1965. This text, unlike many others
more readily available to the general reader, preserves Swift's spelling,
punctuation, and his expressive use of italics. However, since there are
many other editions available I cite quotations by part and chapter
number only (e.g. III, 6). The best annotated edition is Paul Turner's,
Oxford, 1971. The following abbreviations are used throughout:

Prose Works	*The Prose Writings of Jonathan Swift*, ed. Herbert Davis and others, 16 volumes (Blackwell, Oxford, 1939–74).
Tale	*A Tale of a Tub, to which is added The Battle of the Books and the Mechanical Operation of the Spirit*, ed. A. C. Guthkelch and D. Nichol Smith (second edition, Clarendon Press, Oxford, 1958).
Correspondence	*The Correspondence of Jonathan Swift*, ed. Harold Williams, 5 volumes (Clarendon Press, Oxford, 1963–5).
Poems	*The Poems of Jonathan Swift*, ed. Harold Williams, 3 volumes (second edition, Clarendon Press, Oxford, 1958).
Utopia	*The Essential Thomas More*, selected and edited by James J. Greene and John Dolan (Mentor-Omega, New York, Toronto and London, 1967).
Ehrenpreis I–III	Irvin Ehrenpreis, *Swift: The Man, his Works, and the Age*, 3 volumes (Methuen, London, 1962–83).
Nicolson and Mohler	Marjorie Nicolson and Nora M. Mohler, 'The Scientific Background of Swift's *Voyage to Laputa*', *Annals of Science*, II (1937), 405–30, reprinted in A. Norman Jeffares, ed., *Fair Liberty was all his Cry: A Tercentenary Tribute to Jonathan Swift* (Macmillan, London, 1967), pp. 226–69.

1 Introduction
Reading Swift: The Prose Satires

> I am not a little pleased that this Work of mine can possibly meet with no Censurers: For what Objections can be made against a Writer who relates only plain Facts that happened in such distant Countries . . .?
>
> *Gulliver's Travels*, IV, 12

Swift writes for the intelligent reader because his concern is with that most celebrated and abused of human faculties, reason. The nerve centre of his satire lies not only on the printed page but in his reader's ability to discern the treachery of language, the pride of authors, and the reader's own tendency to exempt himself from criticism. We are certain to misread Swift if we assume that there is a simple, stable, and direct relationship between what is written and what Swift himself believes. In all his major prose satires, *A Tale of a Tub*, *Gulliver's Travels*, *A Modest Proposal*, and in many of his poems, the narrator who confronts us may at any moment become the victim of his own writing, slowly and unconsciously submerging in his own confidence. Swift's narrators are wise fools, prone to confess both humble inadequacy and exceptional intelligence. Their common assumption is a sublime conviction that their little book or pamphlet holds the key to the universal improvement of mankind, and that all the reader needs to do is believe in the obvious. This is a sobering caution to anyone who sets out believing he has the 'truth' about Swift.

No truths are ever simple, least of all the 'plain fact' that Swift is, simply, a satirist. Swift's satire is complex, mercurial, paradoxical, and vital. It never stands still. No author vexes his readers more than Swift, and our role as readers is never passive. In the last chapter of *Gulliver's Travels* we are initially addressed as 'Gentle Reader', but this flattery is replaced within a few pages by an awesome and unremitting demolition of human nature as 'a Lump of Deformity, and Diseases both in Body and Mind, smitten with *Pride*'. Gulliver's misanthropic rage has a chilly logical precision which goes far beyond the conventional attack on vices and follies, switching from familiar intimacy to Olympian contempt, and turning the reader from friend to enemy.

Swift's satire is often at its most intense when its speakers plead for honesty, veracity, public spirit, impartiality, reason, intimacy, and 'plain' truths. We expect a satirist to defend truth against lies, honesty against corruption. We should *not* expect a satirist to preach the positives of moral conduct. It is sufficient that errors be exposed. But 'sufficiency' or conventionality are not concepts easily applicable to Swift. He praises by excessive blame and blames by excessive praise: irony is his natural mode of expression, and this demands of his readers a constant sensitivity to tone and expression. For some satirists (Pope and Byron, for example), it may be possible to argue that their strategy is to divide their audience into the victims and the accomplices. The intelligent reader, of course, assumes he or she is in the latter category, a witness to others' follies. But in Swift's satire the ultimate target is the *superior* kind of fool who will, by virtue of his education or social position, exempt himself from the folly of the common herd. Philosophers, theologians, scientists, lawyers, doctors, authors, 'men of Taste', literary critics, the learned, economic theorists, societies for moral reform, and politicians: these are Swift's real villains, those who profess to lead others but whose actions show the delinquency of high authority and the screen for motives of personal aggrandisement. Nor are the downtrodden victims of such leaders exempt from Swift's satire: in his Irish tracts Swift refuses to romanticize the losers; he berates the repressed Irish for helplessly conniving in their own exploitation by England.

Swift's own definition of satire (Author's Preface, *The Battle of the Books*) is surprising. A description of its mechanics is followed by an explanation of its routine failure: *'Satyr is a sort of Glass wherein Beholders do generally discover every Body's Face but their Own which is the chief Reason for that kind of Reception it meets with in the World, and that so very few are offended with it.'* The mirror, not the window, is the optical image Swift prefers. Swift's clear aim is to force the reader to see not only the world's folly reflected in the mirror of satire but also his own contributory role in what seemed to Swift to be the 'ridiculous tragedy' of life. His short poem entitled *The Place of the Damned* (1731) begins with these lines:

> *All folks who pretend to* Religion *and* Grace,
> *Allow there's a* HELL, *but dispute of the place;*

and ends with this couplet:

> *And* HELL *to be sure is at* Paris *or* Rome –
> *How happy for* Us *that it is not at* Home!

Swift's first book, *A Tale of a Tub*, is his most complex. Like Pope's *Dunciad* and Sterne's *Tristram Shandy* it is an image of its own confusion.

Section X of *A Tale* defines three classes of readers: the *Superficial* (prone to laugh), the *Ignorant* (prone to dumb astonishment), and the *Learned* (prone to speculation). Swift's author is determined to curry favour with the *Learned*. Since 'wise Philosophers hold all Writings to be fruitful in the Proportion they are *dark*' (i.e. obscure), an author ambitious to be known must be unintelligible to the common reader. *A Tale* is therefore crammed with pedantic learning, copious allusions, allegory and a zany verbal energy which, in its frenetic search for significant meaning, becomes a principle of randomness. The *form* of the book is both excessive and oppressive (it has an Apology, two dedications, an address from the bookseller to the reader, a preface, an introduction, the Tale itself, nine digressions, and a conclusion), but the *content* escapes. In section IX, 'A Digression on Madness', Swift's narrator generates a theory of history which conflates greatness with madness, so that circumstance only makes the difference between whether a man is seen as a genius or a lunatic. Our author continues:

The present Argument is the most abstracted that ever I engaged in, it strains my Faculties to their highest Stretch; and I desire the Reader to attend with utmost Perpensity; For, I now proceed to unravel this knotty Point.

   ＊THERE is in Mankind a certain＊ ＊ ＊

＊	＊	＊	＊	＊	＊	＊	＊	＊
	＊	＊	＊	＊	＊	＊	＊	＊
Hic multa	＊	＊	＊	＊	＊	＊	＊	
desiderantur	＊	＊	＊	＊	＊	＊	＊	
＊	＊	＊	＊	＊	＊	＊	＊	＊

＊ ＊ ＊ And this I take to be a clear Solution of the
Matter.   (*Tale*, p. 170)

Swift's own footnote, perhaps unnecessarily, points out that the defect in the manuscript is fortunate, since such 'Metaphysical Cobweb Problems' are not worth a solution. Writing about useless questions is a vice of 'Modern' authorship, Swift maintains, and as textual holes open up in *A Tale* the author literally disappears into his own lunatic limbo. The gaps in the manuscript, the unfulfilled promise of sequels, the confessions of a loss of memory and the misplacing of whole sections, all reverse the conventional assumption that the author is in charge of his subject By the end of *A Tale* Swift's author has been written by his own book; a perfect literary image has been created of a mind and a culture bogged down with form, abstract theories, bringing darkness where there once was light. This is only the first instalment in Swift's campaign against the busy 'Modern' minds whose 'converting Imaginations dispose them to reduce all Things into *Types*; who can make *Shadows*, no thanks to the Sun; and then mold them into Substances, no thanks to Philosophy; whose peculiar Talent lies in fixing Tropes and Allegories to the *Letter*, and refining what is Literal into Figure and Mystery'. These are the antecedents of the mad scientists, the projectors, and the cryptographers in the Grand Academy of Lagado in Gulliver's third voyage. Every one of them substitutes the self for the world in an act of proud solipsis, convinced that self-existence is the only certainty and the only value. Similarly, Gulliver ends his four voyages unshakably convinced that his is the only truly rational mind in the human world, and he has the megalomaniac's determination to subdue 'Multitudes to his own *Power*, his *Reasons* or his *Visions*'.

And yet to dismiss the vision of Swift's wise fools is itself a trap for the unwary reader. Swift's narrator in *A Tale* may be mad. Indeed, at the end of 'A Digression on Madness' he admits that his friends think he is only occasionally sane, trusting him to vent his speculations only on useless theories. But a little earlier, and in a paragraph famous for its complexity, Swift's narrator considers the nature and benefits of wisdom in relation to happiness:

In the Proportion that Credulity is a more peaceful Possession of the Mind, than Curiosity, so far preferable is that Wisdom, which converses about the Surface, to that pretended Philosophy which enters into the Depth of Things, and then comes gravely back with Informations and Discoveries, that in the inside they are good for nothing . . . in most Corporeal Beings, which have fallen under my Cognizance, the *Outside* hath been infinitely preferable to the *In*: Whereof I have been farther convinced by some late Experiments. Last week I saw a Woman *flay'd*, and you will hardly believe, how much it altered her Person for the worse. Yesterday I ordered the Carcass of a *Beau* to be stript in my Presence; when we were all amazed to find so many unsuspected Faults under one Suit of Cloaths: Then I laid open his *Brain*, his *Heart*, and his *Spleen*; But, I plainly perceived at every Operation, that the farther we proceeded, we found the Defects encrease upon us in Number and Bulk: from all which, I justly formed this Conclusion to my self; That whatever Philosopher or Projector can find out an Art to sodder and patch up the Flaws and Imperfections of Nature, will deserve much better of Mankind, and teach us a more useful Science, than that so much in present Esteem, of widening and exposing them . . . He that can with *Epicurus* content his Ideas with the *Films* and *Images* that fly off upon his Senses from the *Superficies* of Things; Such a Man truly wise, creams off Nature, leaving the Sower and the Dregs, for Philosophy and Reason to lap up. This is the sublime and refined Point of Felicity, called *the Possession of being well deceived*; The Serene Peaceful State of being a Fool among Knaves.
BUT to return to *Madness*.   (*Tale*, pp. 173–4)

As an image of human corruption there are few more commonplace topics than the whore and the fashionable sensualist. The astonishing quality of this paragraph, however, is its surgically dispassionate, almost bland detachment, and a technique of making a moral commonplace both shocking and vexing. There is no passionate moral denunciation here, and no predictability. The argument that ignorance is preferable to knowledge is part of its point, given the infinity of corruption, but the conclusion suggests that in order to remain socially sane with such knowledge we must acknowledge *both* the moral hopelessness and our own deliberate act of self-delusion. We protect ourselves with an assumed ignorance, and we become accomplices, or at least sleeping partners of corruption. The tone of this paragraph does not suggest that Swift is using irony here, only a bleakly pragmatic anatomy of the conditions of living, and of the manoeuvres we adopt to filter out the recognized but nevertheless intolerable truth. The final sentence in this quotation, 'BUT to return to *Madness*', turns the screw on us. Up to this point we may laugh at the author's ludicrously mechanistic theory of vapours, but can we laugh patronizingly at what he has just told us of our own world? If the role of the satirist is to show the ugly inside of things, to re-focus our superficial complacency, then here, it seems, the satirist (Swift) has chosen to define the limits to honesty and satire through the mind of a crazy narrator. As T. S. Eliot remarked in *Burnt Norton*, 'human kind/Cannot bear very much reality'. Swift gives us only the choice between being a knave or a fool, and there is no authorial signal to show us the path out of this humiliating dilemma.

Swift's texts are like minefields, pre-set with a pattern of explosives hidden from both narrator and reader and detonated by Swift's remote control. Like the terrorist and the modern urban guerrilla Swift wears no easily identifiable uniform. His desire is to infiltrate the enemy's ranks and strike from cover. When the bomb has exploded, Swift himself escapes from the devastation by implicating his narrator-accomplice. A mild example of this technique is in *Verses on the Death of Dr Swift* (1731, pub. 1739), an ostensibly autobiographical poem, where Swift uses an allegedly impartial narrator, one of whose points is that Swift's work was entirely original:

> *His Vein, ironically grave,*
> *Expos'd the Fool, and lash'd the Knave:*
> *To steal a Hint was never known,*
> *But what he writ was all his own.*

> (*Poems*, II, 565, ll. 315–18)

15

But the last two lines are themselves silently plagiarized from another poet's elegy, and it seems that Swift's sub-text undercuts the narrator without at all implying that Swift did indeed steal from others' writing. Swift may be mocking the elegy as a form of uncritical eulogy, he may be mocking elegy-writers, or he may be signalling obliquely a genuine conviction of his own originality. He may be doing all three things at the same time. Whatever the reader decides as to Swift's intentions, the business of critical understanding has been taken out of the hands of the ostensible 'author' and passed indirectly from Swift to the reader. It is a measure of Swift's sometimes dazzling virtuosity that each time his texts are read light gleams from a different angle.

Generally speaking, Swift's satire depends for its success on our recognition of the presence of textual impersonation, or parody. In his own definition (Author's Apology, *A Tale of a Tub*), parodies are 'where the Author personates the Style and Manner of other Writers, whom he has a mind to expose'. Swift offers a comprehensive range of parodic types, all of which are based on degrees of critical re-reading of existing texts or styles. The simplest kind of textual *commentary* is the marginal note. Swift often recorded hostile reactions to books he read by such means. The next stage in recording textual opposition would take the form of a counter-argument, as in his review of Matthew Tindal's deist *Rights of the Christian Church* (1706). Tindal had argued for the separation of Church and State, an argument anathema to Swift, and he accordingly attacked Tindal's work as one of those 'Books that instill pernicious Principles' and tend to 'advance dangerous Opinions, or destroy Foundations'. But Swift evidently tired of a point-by-point rebuttal, abandoned his counter-argument and left the whole project unfinished. Instead, he wrote a brilliant parody of Tindal's *kind* of argument in *An Argument to prove that the Abolishing of Christianity in England, may, as things now stand, be attended with some Inconveniences, and perhaps not produce those many good Effects proposed thereby* (1708). Here Swift attacks what he means to defend and ironically puts up the flimsiest of arguments for the retention of a Christian basis for society. The acid satire in the concluding paragraph additionally exposes the age's sceptical materialism by computing the *economic* danger of abolishing Christianity. Swift is, he admits, not foolish enough to recommend *real* Christianity in such degenerate times, but simply offers a few cautions from within the enemy's own camp:

I do very much apprehend, that in six Months Time, after the Act is passed for the Extirpation of the Gospel, the Bank and *East India* Stock may fall, at least One *per Cent.* And, since that is Fifty Times more than ever the Wisdom of our

Age thought fit to venture for the *Preservation* of Christianity, there is no Reason
we should be at so great a Loss merely for the sake of *destroying* it.

(*Prose Works*, II, 38–9)

The difference between a marginal note and the full-blown parody is
that the latter has completely consumed its target, re-functioning its
style, arguments and literary character, and reproducing a distorted
variant of it. The fact that Swift's *Argument* seems so coolly rational and
logically ordered ironically underlines the dangerous effect of reason
(and materialism) meddling in areas beyond their responsibility and
competence. Parody thus imitates, reconstructs, and eventually oblit-
erates its model, pushing it to the margin of serious attention by ridicule.
Moreover, the alliance of wit and morality, the former brought to the
defence of the latter, reveals another Swiftian characteristic, the simultaneous presence in his work of the preacher and the jester.

Each of Swift's best-known texts is a parody, an image of an already
familiar literary form. With all its formal paraphernalia *A Tale* looks
like a learned book (*The Mechanical Operation of the Spirit* adopts the
then fashionable format of a 'Letter to a Friend'); in 1726 *Gulliver's
Travels* looked like another example of the immensely popular traveller's
tale (complete with maps, nautical jargon, descriptions of foreign
countries, etc.); and *A Modest Proposal* (1729) imitates the economic
tract (its argument being based on statistics, demographic data, and
cost–benefit analysis). In each case Swift copied an existing style of
writing and thinking in order to explode it, and in each case the texts are
written by a pseudonymous author. The only publications which
appeared with Swift's name on the title page in his lifetime, and from his
own pen, were his first publication, *Ode to the Athenian Society* (1692),
the *Proposal for Correcting, Improving, and Ascertaining the English
Tongue* (1722), and the last of *The Drapier's Letters* (1724). Pseudonymity allowed Swift extraordinary artistic freedom, some protection
from prosecution, and the delight of infiltration. Dr Arbuthnot tells the
story best in a letter he wrote to Swift on 5 November 1726, a week after
the publication of *Gulliver's Travels*:

Gulliver is in everybody's hands. Lord Scarborow, who is no inventor of stories,
told me that he fell in company with the master of a ship, who told him that he
was very well acquainted with Gulliver, but that the printer had mistaken, that he
lived in Wapping, and not in Rotherhithe. I lent the book to an old gentleman,
who went immediately to his map to search for Lilly putt.

(*Correspondence*, III, 179–80)

Swift was not out to catch gullible old men, but the circumstantial realism of his literary impersonations provided a central device for his satire on human credulity. The narrator of *A Modest Proposal*, for example, articulates *in his own mind* a philanthropic and socially practicable system to solve Ireland's twin problems of over-population and starvation which depends on infanticide, cannibalism, and racial extermination. The territory between what is proposed by the narrator and what is implied by the real author is occupied by an electrifying irony which draws the reader into the text as witness, judge, victim, and accomplice.

A Modest Proposal offers the clearest example of Swift's parodic methods, and of the way his imagination transformed contemporary sources and experience into savage and immortal satire. Throughout the 1720s Swift had addressed the problem of Ireland's economic, political and moral degradation, largely caused by the mercantilist colonial theory of the Westminster government in England. In constitutional theory England and Ireland were equal under the Crown, but in practice Ireland was treated as a subject colony to be exploited for the exclusive benefit of the 'mother' country. Absentee landlords, forced emigration, punitive trade laws, and political indifference in England all combined to stifle Ireland's development. In the last quarter of the seventeenth century Sir William Petty, the political arithmetician and unofficial surveyor-general of Ireland during the Commonwealth period, wrote at length and in detail on Ireland's plight. His *Treatise of Ireland* (submitted to James II in 1687) put forward an argument to increase the economic value of Ireland to England:

This is to be done. 1. By bringing one Million of the present 1300 Thousand of the People out of Ireland into England, tho' at the Expence of a Million of Money. 2. That the remaining 300 Thousand left behind be all Herdsmen and Dairy-Women, Servants to the Owners of the Lands and Stock Transplanted into England; all aged between 16 and 60 years, and to quit all other Trades, but that of Cattle, and to import nothing but Salt and Tobacco. Neglecting all Housing, but what is fittest for these 300 Thousand People, and this Trade, tho' to the Loss of 2 Millions-worth of Houses. Now if a Million of People be worth 70l. per Head one with another, the whole are worth 70 Millions; then the said People, reckon'd as Money at 5 per Cent. Interest, will yield 3 Millions and a half per Ann. (3). And if Ireland send into England 1 Million and a half worth of Effects (receiving nothing back) Then England will be enriched from Ireland, and otherwise, 5 Millions per Ann. more than now: Which, at 20 Year's Purchase, is worth one Hundred Millions of Pounds Sterling, as was propounded . . .*

If human beings can thus be reduced to commodities, it is a short step to the production of people as food. Swift's modest proposer recommends

* Sir William Petty, 'An Essay in Political Arithmetic', in his *Treatise of Ireland* (1687); see C. H. Hull (ed.), *The Economic Writings of Sir William Petty*, 2 vols., Cambridge, 1899, II, 574.

the eating of babies in his tenth paragraph, having carefully established that in the modern world children are already sold and, in America, it seems, eaten at twelve months old. The bitter irony behind this cruel fantasy is directed at the politicians, whose actions or indifference have created a problem resistant to all 'normal' attempts at amelioration. It is they who must ask 'the Parents of these Mortals, whether they would not at this Day think it a great Happiness to have been sold for Food at a year Old, in the manner I prescribe; and thereby have avoided such a perpetual Scene of Misfortunes, as they have since gone through, by the *oppression of Land-lords*, the Impossibility of paying Rent without Money or Trade, the want of common Sustenance, with neither House nor Cloaths to cover them from Inclemences of Weather, and the most inevitable Prospect of intailing the like, or greater Miseries upon their Breed for ever'. This overt moral challenge to Ireland's oppressors carries indignation and rage at an injustice which has become an 'accepted' institution. But Swift knew that such an appeal would be sterile. How much more effective, then, to use the language of the profit-seeking capitalist in combination with an ultimate taboo? If yet another 'economic' argument would be ignored, moral shock-tactics might succeed as in the seventh and subsequent paragraphs of *A Modest Proposal*:

I am assured by our Merchants, that a Boy or Girl before twelve Years old, is no saleable Commodity; and even when they come to this Age, they will not yield above Three Pounds, or Three Pounds and half a Crown at most, on the Exchange; which cannot turn to Account either to the Parents or the Kingdom; the Charge of Nutriment and Rags, having been at least four Times that Value.

I shall now therefore humbly propose my own Thoughts; which I hope will not be liable to the least Objection.

I have been assured by a very knowing *American* of my Acquaintance in *London*; that a young healthy Child, well nursed, is, at a Year old, a most delicious, nourishing, and wholesome Food; whether *Stewed, Roasted, Baked,* or *Boiled*; and, I make no doubt, that it will equally serve in a *Fricasie*, or *Ragoust*.

I do therefore humbly offer it to *publick Consideration*, that of the Hundred and Twenty Thousand Children, already computed, Twenty thousand may be reserved for Breed; whereof only one Fourth Part to be Males; which is more than we allow to *Sheep, black Cattle,* or *Swine*; and my Reason is, that these Children are seldom the Fruits of Marriage, a *Circumstance not much regarded by our Savages*; therefore, *one Male* will be sufficient to serve *four Females*. That the remaining Hundred thousand, may, at a Year old, be offered in Sale to the *Persons of Quality* and *Fortune*, through the Kingdom; always advising the Mother to let them suck plentifully in the last Month, so as to render them plump, and fat for a good Table. A Child will make two Dishes at an Entertainment for Friends; and when the Family dines alone, the fore or hind Quarter will make a reasonable Dish; and seasoned with a little Pepper or Salt, will be very good Boiled on the Fourth Day, especially in *Winter*.

In his *Answer to the Craftsman* (*c.* 1730), Swift returned to the detached tone and quantitative manner of the economist in order to obliterate (and hence cry out for) a *human* response:

These Eight Thousand Four Hundred Families may be divided among the four Provinces, according to the Number of Houses in each Province; and making the equal Allowance of Eight to a Family, the Number of Inhabitants will amount to Sixty Seven Thousand Two Hundred Souls; to these we are to add a Standing Army of Twenty Thousand *English*, which, together with their Trulls, their Bastards, and their Horse-boys, will, by gross Computation, very near double the Count, and be very near sufficient for the Defence and grazing of the Kingdom, as well as to enrich our Neighbours, expel Popery, and keep out the Pretender.

(*Prose Works*, XII, 175–6)

In *A Modest Proposal* the Irish do not simply die, they perish; they are not merely exploited, they are enslaved. The proposer's humanitarianism is 'proven' when he suggests that the proportion of children reserved for breed should be *greater* than that for '*Sheep, black Cattle*, or *Swine*', and his motives are purely 'disinterested' as he concludes that he has published his proposal for '*the public Good of my Country, by advancing our Trade, providing for Infants, relieving the Poor, and giving some Pleasure to the Rich. I have no Children, by which I can propose to get a single Penny; the youngest being nine Years old, and my Wife past Childbearing.*' Everything the proposer says is subject to an alternative and opposite interpretation, but Swift leaves the obvious unsaid, assuming his reader can savour the cruel comedy for himself, and note how the pride of this patriotic do-gooder masks the perpetration of an evil greater than the cause of his own private anguish. In such writing we glimpse more than Swift's own rage at injustice and suffering, that 'savage indignation' which he had engraved on his epitaph; we can also see a fundamental scepticism at work. This is not a conviction of the utter hopelessness of things, for if this were the case Swift would not have spent his life battling for liberty. On the contrary, it is a *philosophic* conviction that there are clear and permanent limits set to man's perfectibility, that the idealist who proposes elegant abstract solutions to essentially human moral problems is at best an admirable fool and at worst a self-seeking villain.

2 Life and Critical After-life

The last Thing I shall take notice of, that some raise against us, is, That *Ireland* is to be look'd upon only as a *Colony* from *England*: And therefore as the Roman *Colonies* were subject to, and bound by, the Laws made by the *Senate* at *Rome*; so ought *Ireland* by those made by the *Greater Council* at *Westminster*. Of all the Objections rais'd against us, I take this to be the most extravagant; it seems not to have the least *Foundation* or *Colour* from *Reason* or *Record*: Does it not manifestly appear by the *Constitution* of *Ireland*, that 'tis a *Compleat Kingdom* within itself?

William Molyneux, *The Case of Ireland* (1697/8)

Going to England is a very good thing, if it were not attended with an ugly circumstance of returning to Ireland.

Swift to Pope, 17 November 1726

You say that Ireland is a millstone about our necks; that it would be better for us if Ireland were sunk at the bottom of the sea; that the Irish are a race of irreclaimable savages and barbarians. How often have I heard these sentiments fall from the plump and thoughtless squire, and from the thriving English shopkeeper, who has never felt the rod of an Orange master upon his back.

Sydney Smith, *Letters ... on the Catholics*, VI (1808)

Swift's life, for better or worse, was interwoven with the fortunes of Ireland and its ambiguous relationship with England. Ireland was to provide both his living as a clergyman and his political base as a writer. It was also to provide him with a satirical detachment from which to expose the iniquities of English colonialism, its moral indifference to the fate of John Bull's other island, and its intolerance. 'What I did for this Country', he wrote, 'was from perfect Hatred of Tyranny and Oppression' (*Prose Works*, XIII, 111). And yet Swift's own relationship with Ireland was profoundly ambiguous. He could neither love it as a native Irishman, nor could he wholly despise or remain indifferent to it for as long as his acute sense of injustice was provoked by its repression.

In Swift's time Ireland was not divided by frontiers we can identify on a map. Divisions within it were nevertheless deep and complex. The partition of Ireland in 1922 into Ulster and Southern Ireland recognized already endemic differences in religion and political loyalties between a relatively recently arrived but dominant Protestant minority in the north, and an overwhelmingly Catholic majority in the south. Dublin in the eighteenth century was the national centre, its parliament being a colonial instrument subject to the English parliament at Westminster. Ireland was unique in Western Europe in that the persecuted formed the majority of the population. Anti-Catholic laws excluded this majority from parliament, government office, the legal profession, and the armed services. The exclusion was achieved by prescribing a religious test for all aspirants to public office which no committed Catholic could take, such as professing disbelief in the doctrine of substantiation and condemnation of the worship of Mary and the saints as 'superstitious and idolatrous'. Legislation passed in 1704 and in 1709 forbade Catholics from buying land and from leasing it for longer than thirty-one years. By 1778 less than five per cent of land was left in Catholic hands. The native Irish Catholic peasantry had to pay tithes to the (Anglican) Church of Ireland. Although Henry VIII had become King of Ireland in 1541, the first to bear such a title, the Reformation had failed to establish Protestantism in Ireland. Its subsequent history is that of a colony strictly controlled by a power structure which owed its identity and its allegiances to England. Even though Ireland remained a Catholic country (and largely *because* of this fact), the reins of political, ecclesiastical, and civil powers were in the hands of the 'English interest'. Swift remarked in his *Short View of Ireland*, 'we are in the Condition of Patients who have their Physick sent them by Doctors at a Distance, Strangers to their Constitution, and the Nature of their Disease'. And this was from a leading member of the Anglo-Irish Protestant Ascendancy safely located within the Anglican Pale of sophisticated Dublin! The 'Physick' included a series of legislative acts of the English parliament dating from the 1690s designed to restrict the Irish economy (in particular its trade in wool and cattle) and enforce its dependence on the 'mother' country.

Stresses within Ireland were, broadly speaking, tripartite, between the Anglo-Irish Protestants (for whom Swift spoke), the native Catholic Irish majority (whose civil and religious rights Swift could not recognize), and the Presbyterian dissenters descended from the Scottish migrants of the early seventeenth century (whose fanaticism he deplored). Catholic rebellions occurred in 1641 and in 1689 (the latter sending Swift and many others to England). It was not until 1652 that Cromwell's armies 'pacified' Ireland with a reign of terror and wave of property expropriation specifically directed against the Catholic population. Royalist Anglicans also suffered, and Swift told with pride the story of his grandfather's loyalist suffering under the Parliamentarian regime. Irishmen found disloyal to England faced death, loss of property, or both; many Irish Catholics were transported or reduced to beggary. Around the time of the Restoration in 1660 Swift's father moved to the newly pacified Ireland in search of advancement, settled into a well-established Dublin parish known for its legal character, and created a new life determined by English loyalties. In 1685 the Catholic James II's policies raised new hopes in Ireland that the balance of power would shift away from Protestant domination. A Declaration of Indulgence was issued in 1687, suspending the Test Acts and granting liberty of worship to Protestant and Catholic dissenters, and the Attainder Act offered a largely Catholic resettlement of Ireland. The Earl of Tyrconnel set about replacing Protestant appointees with Catholics in the army, the judiciary, in corporations, and in the university. Trinity College Dublin began to empty, and Protestants (mostly merchants) took themselves and their money out of Ireland. Swift's seven-year period of study there came to an end by January 1689. In England the revolution of 1688 had replaced James with the Protestant William III. In his own words, and beginning with a phrase that was to haunt Irish history ever since, Swift wrote: 'The troubles then breaking out, he went to his mother in Leicester, and after continuing there some months . . . was received by Sir William Temple.'

Swift thus came from, and was repeatedly to return to, a country both internally divided and externally repressed. No group within it could feel confidence in the protection and support of the English government. England provided Swift with a means to escape from the violence of 1688–9, but as one of the founders of Irish Protestant nationalism he also saw that Ireland's problems were a direct consequence of England's colonial tyranny. Swift belonged to an oligarchy which held the land, the civic power, and the keys to all advancement. A recurrent strain in Swift's letters to his close friends in England is how little was understood of Ireland's situation across St George's Channel (also known as the Irish Sea). Yet Swift was not the only voice raised in protest. The *de facto* leader of the Anglo-Irish opposition to the 'English interest' in Dublin was Swift's ecclesiastical superior, the Dean of St Patrick's, William King (1650–1729). King was an Irishman, a Whig, and intolerant of both Presbyterian dissenters and Catholics alike. It was King who sent Swift to London to negotiate the remission of ecclesiastical taxes, and who supported Swift's campaign against Wood's Ha'pence.* He was also a staunch opponent of England's policy of preferring Englishmen in the Church of Ireland. In 1691 he argued his anti-Catholic and pro-revolutionary case in *The State of the Protestants of Ireland under the late King James's Government*, based on materials he had collected during his imprisonment in Dublin Castle by the Jacobite government. Both King and Swift were influenced by William

* See pages 43–44 below.

Molyneux's classic anti-mercantilist work, *The Case of Ireland's being bound by Acts of Parliament in England stated* (1698). Molyneux (1656–1698) was the founding secretary of the Dublin Philosophical Society (1683), a friend, disciple, and correspondent of John Locke, and in his *Case* argued that Ireland could not be bound by laws made in England without its free consent. Swift was to adopt Molyneux's arguments in his own *Drapier's Letters*, pointedly identifying 'the famous Mr Molineux' as 'an *English* Gentleman born here'.

Swift was born on 30 November 1667, seven years after the restoration of Charles II, and died in the year of the Jacobite Rebellion, 1745. He was twenty-seven when the 'Glorious Revolution' in England toppled the Catholic James II and replaced him with the Protestant William III. Swift's parents were English Dublin Protestants, members of the middle-class Anglican community living within an enclave surrounded by an overwhelmingly Catholic population. Swift's father died seven or eight months before Jonathan was born. His early education, first at Kilkenny College and subsequently (from 1682) at Trinity College Dublin, was the best available in Ireland at the time, although Swift later denigrated it. His academic career was undistinguished, and after graduation by *special grace* in 1686 he was employed by the retired diplomat Sir William Temple, first at Sheen (June 1689), and then at Moor Park in Surrey (August 1691), where he became the tutor to the eight-year-old Esther Johnson (Stella). Swift lived at Moor Park from 1689 to 1690, 1691 to 1694, and from 1696 until Temple's death in January 1699. The first of several interruptions in this ten-year residence occurred in July 1690, when Swift crossed to Ireland in search of preferment, returning as Temple's secretary and literary executor in August 1691. Between May 1694 and May 1696 Swift was the ordained priest in Kilroot, in the diocese of Down and Connor, a strongly dissenting area. Here he would have gained first-hand experience of Irish nonconformism, and materials for the satire on the Dissenting Jack in *A Tale of a Tub*. In Temple's household, by contrast, he could immerse himself in the humanist learning of an Anglican and Royalist cultural tradition. He also learned from Temple's disillusioned retirement about the fickle nature of a political career. Between 1696 and 1699 he wrote *The Battle of the Books*, a loyal defence of Temple's shaky scholarship against the 'Modern' scholarship of William Wotton and Richard Bentley. Swift here described Temple as 'the greatest Champion' of the Ancients, even though Bentley (a prodigious classical scholar) had demonstrated Temple's blunder in literary attribution. Most of *A Tale of a Tub* was also written at this time and, together with *The Mechanical Operation of*

the Spirit (a further attack on spiritual and intellectual fanaticism), all
three pieces were published anonymously in 1704. After Temple's death
Swift returned to Dublin as domestic chaplain to the Earl of Berkeley
(newly appointed Lord Justice). He was granted the vicarage of Laracor,
near Dublin, and a prebend in St Patrick's Cathedral. Berkeley was
recalled to England in 1701 and Swift returned with him. He transcribed
and edited three volumes of Temple's *Letters* for publication in 1701 and
1703. *Contests and Dissensions . . . in Athens and Rome*, a defence of the
Whigs under the guise of 'parallel' (Athenian) history, appeared in 1701,
as did the magnificent comic poem *Mrs Frances Harris's Petition*. In the
same year he returned to Ireland, and transcribed and edited Temple's
Miscellanea (volumes II and III). In 1702 he graduated Doctor of
Divinity from Trinity College, and Esther Johnson and Rebecca Dingley
took up residence in Dublin.

After the accession of Queen Anne (1702) Swift's political career was
determined by the fortunes of the Tories. In 1707 he was appointed a
commissioner of the Church of Ireland to negotiate (successfully) with
the Whig government in London the remission of the First Fruits (ecclesiastical taxes levied on the Irish clergy). The actual legislation remitting
the taxes was established not by the Whigs but later by Robert Harley,
for whom Swift was to write as propagandist in the Tory *Examiner*
papers. From this period dates his friendship with Addison and Steele
and his intimacy with the passionate Esther Vanhomrigh (then aged
twenty and the Vanessa of *Cadenus and Vanessa*). Having published the
Bickerstaff Papers and the third and final volume of Temple's *Memoirs*
between 1708 and 1709, Swift returned to Ireland. In October 1710 the
Tories were swept into office and Swift began to write for the new
Harley ministry. A minute account of Swift's social and political activities
at the centre of cultural and political life in London is recorded in his
correspondence with Esther Johnson, known as the *Journal to Stella*.
From 2 November 1710 to 14 June 1711 Swift wrote thirty-three *Ex-*
aminer papers. *The Conduct of the Allies*, directed against the Whig
policy of continuing the protracted War of the Spanish Succession
against France, was published in November 1711. Harley was appointed
Earl of Oxford and Lord Treasurer, but a mutual hostility developed
between Oxford and Henry St John (Secretary, and later Viscount
Bolingbroke), which steadily worsened. In 1713 Swift wrote *Cadenus and*
Vanessa, a justification of his conduct towards Esther Vanhomrigh and
an attempt to control her passion for him. In the same year he was
installed as Dean of St Patrick's Cathedral, Dublin (*English* episcopal
appointments were under the control of Queen Anne, and Swift was

never to be entrusted with such eminence). In London in 1713 Swift was a leading member of the Scriblerus Club, a loose confederacy of Tory wits including Pope, Oxford, Bolingbroke, Parnell, Arbuthnot, Gay and others, dedicated to campaigning against dulness in cultural life. Their campaign was, however obscurely, responsible for the eventual appearance of *Gulliver's Travels* (1726), Gay's *The Beggar's Opera* (1728), Pope's *Dunciad* (1728 and 1743), and the collaborative and incomplete *Memoirs of Martinus Scriblerus* (1741), a mock-biography of a dunce.

In July 1714 the Tory ministry of Oxford and Bolingbroke collapsed and Swift retired temporarily to Letcombe Regis in Berkshire. After Queen Anne's death Oxford was imprisoned in the Tower and Bolingbroke fled to the Pretender's court in France, accused of Jacobitism (he abandoned the Pretender in 1716, received the royal pardon in 1723 and resettled in England in 1725). George I and the Whigs assumed power and Swift returned to Dublin on 16 August 1714. Here he turned his attention to Irish pamphleteering, a long-range assault on the English government. The first round came with *A Proposal for the Universal Use of Irish Manufacture* (1720), and soon after we learn of the first mention of the composition of *Gulliver's Travels*, in many ways an allegory of his political experiences from 1702 to 1714 and beyond. Vanessa died in 1723 and a year later *The Drapier's Letters* (I–V, March to December 1724) made Swift a hero of the Irish resistance to England's domination of its economy. Two years later, on 6 March 1726, Swift arrived in London carrying a manuscript of *Gulliver's Travels*. He stayed for four months, mostly with Pope at Twickenham, and his masterpiece was published from a fair copy (probably not in Swift's hand) by Benjamin Motte on 28 October 1726, after Swift had returned to Dublin. Much to Swift's anger and dismay, the book was published in a 'mangled' and partly censored form, probably the work of the Reverend Andrew Tooke, a sleeping partner in Motte's firm. One of several omissions was Swift's allegorical account of Irish resistance to Wood's Ha'pence in I I, 3. The year 1727 saw Swift's last visit to England (for about six months), before his return to Dublin and the death of Stella (28 January 1727/8). *A Modest Proposal* appeared in 1729, and Swift received the Freedom of the city of Dublin. *Verses on the Death of Dr Swift* was written in 1731, and in 1735 Swift's Dublin printer George Faulkner published a four-volume edition of Swift's collected works including the corrected edition of *Gulliver's Travels*. On 17 August 1742 Swift was declared 'of unsound mind and memory' (his actual disability, not diagnosed until 1861, was bilateral Ménière's disease, a disabling ailment of the middle ear leading to dizziness, head-noises, nausea and deafness), and he died on 19

October 1745 in the Deanery. His will included a provision of £11,000 for the establishment of a hospital for the insane, the St Patrick's Hospital which exists to this day. In 1758 his *History of the Four Last Years of the·Queen* was published posthumously.

The paradoxes and tensions in Swift's life are both clear and numerous: of English background and Irish birth, a Church of England man in a Catholic country, a leader of the Anglo-Irish Protestant ascendancy whose most intense friendship was with the Catholic Alexander Pope and with the Jacobite Bolingbroke. Denied preferment in England (perhaps through court suspicion of his less than vigorous defence of the Church of England in *A Tale of a Tub*), he was sent to defend the frontiers of Anglicanism in a colony. In his own mind Ireland was a place of punitive exile, but he turned it into an indictment of England. Of English cultural loyalties, but a passionate political opponent of its policies after 1714, he was compromised by his political brief to repress the native Irish demand for civil rights and his complex personal loyalty to human liberty. A willing client and beneficiary of Sir William Temple's aristocratic patronage and cultural values, he was nevertheless fiercely independent, nobody's political puppet, and a man whose immense ambition to leave his own mark on the world derived from an early sense of exclusion and disappointment. In 1729 Swift wrote to Pope and Bolingbroke:

I remember, when I was a little boy, I felt a great fish at the end of my line, which I drew up almost on the ground, but it dropt in, and the disappointment vexeth me to this day, and I believe it was the type of all my future disappointments . . . I am ashamed to tell you, that when I was very young I had more desire to be famous than ever since; and fame, like all things else in this life, grows with me every day more a trifle . . . all my endeavours from a boy to distinguish my self, were only from want of a great Title and Fortune, that I might be used like a Lord by those who have an opinion of my parts; whether right or wrong, it is no great matter; and so the reputation of wit or great learning does the office of a blue riband, or of a coach and six horses.   (*Correspondence*, III, 329–30)

The power of Swift's writing is frequently like that of a tyrant over a minion, knocking over by patrician contempt the feeble attempt to ingratiate and placate a social superior. We witness this dominance in the King of Brobdingnag, and in Gulliver's final chapter. It is also a structural principle in Swift's own technique of trapping his characters in a posture of ingratiating deference to the reader and a simultaneous sublime arrogance in relation to the world itself. In George Orwell's words, Swift was 'a Tory anarchist, despising authority while believing

27

in liberty, and preserving the aristocratic outlook while seeing clearly that the existing aristocracy is degenerate and contemptible'. In *Gulliver's Travels* we can glimpse the frustration of a brilliant outsider who has interpreted his exclusion as the sign of a radically corrupt social and moral order; and in his life (as in *Gulliver's Travels*) we can discern the themes of early separation and loss marked subsequently by intense personal loyalties, beginning with Temple, his mentor and patron, and then with Arbuthnot, Gay, Pope (his intellectual peers), Harley and Bolingbroke (his political masters), and with Esther and Vanessa, two women in whose relationship with Swift there is starkly revealed Swift's need for companionable female intimacy which stops short at sexual commitment.

In Ireland Swift felt trapped in a 'theatre in a barn'; it was 'the land I hate' controlled by perfidious Albion. *The Holyhead Journal* (1727) speaks clearly of Swift's sardonic helplessness in Ireland, a country, in the later words of Sydney Smith (*Edinburgh Review*, 1820), 'more barbarous than the rest of Europe, because it has been worse treated and more cruelly oppressed':

> *Remove me from this land of slaves*
> *Where all are fools, and all are knaves*
> *Where every knave & fool is bought,*
> *Yet kindly sells himself for nought*
> *Where Whig and Tory fiercely fight*
> *Who's in the wrong, who in the right*
> *And where their country lyse at stake*
> *They only fight for fighting sake,*
> *While English sharpers take the pay,*
> *And then stand by to see fair play.*

Swift's after-life, i.e. the image of him created by his readers and critics, testifies to the sheer power of his writing. It has often been characterized by fabulous distortions. All the nonsense written about his alleged 'secret marriage' to Stella, the pathological basis of his satire, his 'madness' and his misanthropy, is evidence of the critic's fascination for, and sometimes need for revenge on, a writer who refuses to fit into decorous niceties. One of Swift's maxims runs: 'There are but three ways for a man to revenge himself of a censorious world. To despise it; to return the like; or to endeavour to live so as to avoid it. The first of these is usually pretended; the last is almost impossible; the universal practice is for the second.' The keen critical irony of Swift's reputation is that his caustic analysis of human idiocy was to be turned against him. Samuel Johnson, prompted by a reading of the fourth voyage of Gulliver, first raised suspicions about Swift's 'obsession' with filth and nastiness, yet it was also Johnson who declared a Swiftian scepticism in *Rasselas* (1759): 'Of the uncertainties of our present state, the most dreadful and alarming is the uncertain continuance of reason . . ., Perhaps, if we speak with rigorous exactness, no human mind is in its right state . . . All power of fancy over reason is a degree of insanity.' In the nineteenth century Thackeray intensified the suspicion of a pathological 'explanation' for Swift's satire, and told his polite readers not to read Gulliver's fourth voyage; R. L. Stevenson thought of Swift as a human goat, 'leaping and wagging his scut on mountains of offence'; George Orwell, one of Swift's shrewdest critics, thought that Swift, like Tolstoy, shows 'a sort of horror of the actual process of life', even though *Gulliver's Travels* would be one of the six books preserved by Orwell if all others were to be destroyed. He further noted that *Gulliver's Travels* shows that 'if the force of belief is behind it, a world-view which only just passes the test of sanity is sufficient to produce a great work of art' (*Shooting an Elephant and Other Essays*, 1950). Leaving aside the question of whether Swift's or the world's sanity is at issue, and neglecting the fundamental strategies of Swift as a *satirist*, F. R. Leavis noted Swift's 'peculiar emotional intensity . . . probably the most remarkable expression of negative feelings and attitudes that literature can offer – the spectacle of creative powers . . . exhibited consistently in negation and rejection . . . the channels of life have been blocked and perverted' ('The Irony of Swift', *Determinations*, 1934). James Agee observed in *Let Us Now Praise Famous Men* (1941) a worse fate than critical denigration: 'Swift, Blake, Beethoven, Christ, Joyce, Kafka, name me a one who has not been . . . castrated. Official acceptance is the one unmistakable symptom that salvation is beaten again, and is the one surest sign of fatal misunderstanding, and is the kiss of Judas.' In no other writer's work is it clearer than in the case of Swift that the critic constructs an image of the work after the prejudices and requirements of his own mind. Norman O. Brown's revisionary chapter on Swift ('The Excremental Vision'), in *Life Against Death: The Psychoanalytical Meaning of History* (1959) exposed both some literary criticism and some psychoanalysis to a latter-day Swiftian mirror, reflecting either prim and superior censorship as the motive, or a pompous moral custodianship of literature and readership. Brown cites one psychoanalyst's report on Swift written as though literature were simply documents in an individual case-history:

It is submitted on the basis of such a study of *Gulliver's Travels* that Swift was a neurotic who exhibited psychosexual infantilism, with a particular showing of coprophilia, associated with misogyny, misanthropy, mysophilia and mysophobia.

(p. 182)

In finding 'startling anticipations of Freudian theorems about anality, about sublimation, and about the universal neurosis of mankind' in Swift's *wit*, this influential essay, ironically, returned to an earlier metaphor for Swift's genius, his literary imagination. It also paid Swift the compliment of knowing what he was writing about, and laid to rest the persistent romantic myth that literature is no more than an individual confession. The disentangling of Swiftian myths from Swiftian facts still confronted the most recent,* and definitive, biography of Swift. The first volume of Irvin Ehrenpreis's *Swift: The Man, his Works, and the Age* (3 volumes, 1962–83) opens thus:

Here, neither Swift nor Stella is made a bastard; Swift does not say, 'My uncle gave me the education of a dog'; Dryden does not say, 'Cousin Swift, you will never be a poet'; and Temple does not seat Swift and Stella at the servants' table.

(I, ix)

When the reader is freed from such legends, he finds that there are sufficient puzzles and paradoxes in what Swift wrote to occupy a lifetime. In the words of W. B. Yeats, 'Swift haunts me; he is always just around the next corner.'

* For a shorter account, see David Nokes, *Jonathan Swift, A Hypocrite Reversed: A Critical Biography*, Clarendon Press, Oxford, 1985.

3   Gulliver's Travels

It is difficult to say with any precision when the idea of *Gulliver's Travels* first came to Swift. Although most of it was written between the years 1720 and 1725, the prefatory list of promised works in *A Tale* includes 'A Voyage into *England*, by a Person of Quality in *Terra Australis incognita*, translated from the Original'. Whatever Swift's original intention may have been, and here he seems to have been thinking of a particular device of using an *outsider* to examine the *familiar*, the final result was directly opposite. He was to parody the *genuine* traveller's tale by taking an ordinary Englishman to exotic and fantastic places, testing his normality against the bizarre. Many years after the publication of the *Travels*, in the jointly-authored and incomplete *Memoirs of Martinus Scriblerus* (1741) there is a sly synopsis of the *Travels* (chapter XVI) which makes clear the satirical perspective we are to take on Gulliver himself. The first voyage of Martinus Scriblerus was 'to a Discovery of the ancient *Pygmaean* Empire ... in his second, he was as happily shipwreck'd on the Land of the *Giants*, now the most humane people in the world ... in his third Voyage, he discover'd a whole Kingdom of *Philosophers*, who govern by the *Mathematicks* ... in his fourth Voyage he discovers a Vein of Melancholy proceeding almost to a Disgust of his species; but above all, a mortal Detestation to the whole flagitious Race of *Ministers*, and a final Resolution not to give in any *Memorial* to the *Secretary of State*, in order to subject the Lands he discover'd to the *Crown* of *Great Britain*'. The next paragraph hints further at the improbability of a ship's surgeon, and later captain of a merchantman, acting the role of a 'Philosopher, a Politician, and a Legislator', and the final paragraph undercuts the famous hero by some heavy ironic praise:

And whoever he be, that shall farther observe, in every page of such a book, that cordial *Love of Mankind*, that *inviolable Regard* to *Truth*, that *Passion* for his *dear Country*, and that particular attachment to the excellent Princess Queen *Anne*; surely that man deserves to be pitied, if by all those visible Signs and Characters, he cannot distinguish and acknowledge the Great *Scriblerus*.

Gulliver is thus retrospectively associated by the Scriblerian group with the dabbling intellectual inanities of Martinus Scriblerus the 'Universal Artist' and 'Prodigy of our Age'. We are explicitly invited to think twice before we accept Gulliver's earnest expressions of his own veracity and 'authenticity' in a genre legendary for its fantastic inventions. Swift, of course, pursues the opposite track, making the fictional Gulliver as real as possible. He is the cousin of William Dampier (1652–1715), whose *New Voyage Round the World* had been published in 1697, a book to which *Gulliver's Travels* bears a strong physical resemblance. Towards the end of the fourth voyage Gulliver alludes to his 'worthy Friend', the famous Dutch cartographer Hermann Moll, whose maps of the world (and of Australia in particular) were to be copied by Swift's illustrators. Like Defoe's *Robinson Crusoe* (1719), *Gulliver's Travels* is carefully crafted to look like the authentic account of an individual experience, at least for the first few pages.

There were many precedents, analogues and sources available to Swift in the 1720s for a mock-traveller's tale. A standard classical education would have made Lucian's *True History* (*c.* 170 A.D.) familiar, and readers would savour the parallel between Gulliver's encounter with Alexander the Great, Hannibal, Caesar and Brutus in the magical island of Glubbdubdrib, and Lucian's account of the meeting between Socrates, Homer and Plato. Francis Godwin imitated Lucian in his thirty-page fantasy, *Voyage of Domingo Gonzales, or The Man in the Moon* (1638), as did Cyrano de Bergerac in his *Histoire Comique de la Lune* (1657). Fontenelle's philosophical dialogue on the question of life on other planets appeared in 1686 as *Entretiens sur la Pluralité des Mondes*, and other moon-fictions included John Wilkins's *The Discovery of a World in the Moone* (1638) and Defoe's *The Consolidator* (1705), an early example of space fiction which includes a lunar language. Swift combined such fantasies with ingredients taken from real voyages, such as Dampier's, and from the grotesque satiric fiction of Rabelais' *Gargantua and Pantagruel* (1547). Rabelais' court of Queen Whim (Book V, chapters xxi–xxii) is a precursor of Swift's Academy of Lagado, and so is the Academy in Joseph Hall's *Mundus Alter et Idem* (1610). The method by which Gulliver extinguishes the palace fire in I, 5 recalls Gargantua causing a flood in the Paris street by the same action. The parallels and echoes between works in this extremely fluid category of imaginary/philosophic/parody voyages are numberless. Of greater importance is the category of high-toned philosophical analysis of society stemming from Plato's *Republic* and, of peculiar significance to Swift himself, Sir Thomas More's *Utopia* (1516), discussed in more detail below.

Swift evidently found in the imaginary voyage a perfect vehicle for analysing what is essentially a simple if permanent paradox of human experience: the urge to find in the imagination a better world than exists in actuality, together with the foolish belief that imaginative constructs could *replace* the imperfect world. Much of *Gulliver's Travels*, its comedy and its moral outrage, straddles this dilemma, and as we follow Gulliver's increasing disillusion with his own world it is best to remember Swift's own remark that life was in essence a combination of grandeur *and* humiliation, aspiration *and* dejection: 'The common saying of life being a Farce, is true in every sense but the most important one, for it is a ridiculous tragedy, which is the worst kind of composition' (*Correspondence*, IV, 456). In the *Travels* he produced a permanent reminder of the tragic farce of human perception. It may have begun with comedy, but it finished with something else. Back in 1711 Swift had written to Stella that he had provided Joseph Addison with a 'noble hint' for *Spectator* No. 50, which purported to be an extract from a journal kept by four Iroquois chiefs who had (in fact) visited London in 1710. Their baffled accounts of a 'monstrous Kind of Animals' (Whigs and Tories), strange costumes and inexplicable cave-like structures (St Paul's Cathedral), turn upside down the Eurocentric normalities. In a genuine domestic travel-book of the time, John Macky states in his popular *Journey through England* (1714): 'Every English gentleman of condition ought to go abroad, to see the miseries of the enslaved part of the world, in order to give him a better taste and value for the constitution of his own country' (I, vi). Swift's residence in Ireland could only sharpen his already keen sense of patriotic myopia and insular prejudice. We need only recall Gulliver's words in the final chapter to see what Swift does with this particular imperialist trope: 'instead of Proposals for conquering that magnanimous Nation [the Houyhnhnms], I rather wish they were in a Capacity or Disposition to send a sufficient Number of their Inhabitants for civilizing *Europe*; by teaching us the first Principles of Honour, Justice, Truth, Temperance, publick Spirit, Fortitude, Chastity, Friendship, Benevolence, and Fidelity'.

i Big Men and Little Men: Parts I and II

Dr Johnson's remark about the facile imaginative structure of *Gulliver's Travels* seems perverse when we consider how closely the first and second voyages are connected, and how fundamental the difference is between the first two and the last two voyages. Boswell expressed his astonishment:

> Johnson was in high spirits this evening at the club, and talked with great animation and success. *The Tale of a Tub* is so much superior to his other

writings, that one can hardly believe he was the author of it. 'There is in it such a vigour of mind, such a swarm of thoughts, so much of nature, and art, and life.' I wondered to hear him say of *Gulliver's Travels*, 'When once you have thought of big men and little men, it is very easy to do all the rest.'

(Life of Johnson, 24 March 1775)

On the contrary, it has seemed to most readers that the comedy of relativities (at least of size and perception) is perhaps the easiest and smoothest part of Swift's book, and that the third and fourth parts are different in kind, less predictable in their comic rationale; that the third part is scattered and multifarious in its subjects and effect; and that the fourth part rises to a crescendo of moral intensity and intellectual difficulty without parallel in anything Swift ever wrote. In his *Life of Swift* Johnson is more specific. His mind evidently 'shrinks with disgust' at the fourth voyage, about which he enquired: 'what has disease, deformity, and filth, upon which the thoughts can be allured to dwell'. In highlighting the first two voyages, Johnson was also saying that he would rather not think at all about the fourth. Twentieth-century Swift criticism has been engrossed by it.

Gulliver's Travels is a mixed satire. Beginning as a traveller's tale, it ends as a moral sermon, and throughout the four voyages the reader peers at Gulliver through sub-textual frameworks of utopian/dystopian satire, political allegory, fictional biography, and myth, strung together by a Gulliver who is, variously, an 'autonomous' character, often the average representative of his culture, sometimes the victim of his own (and Swift's) strategies, and finally a self-righteous preacher alienated from his own species. In other words, Gulliver is not a character from whom we should expect a psychological consistency but an element in a total and not always coherent satirical argument. Swift's book may be read as an enjoyable fantasy in its own right, and countless versions for children have been published making everything of the fantasy and nothing of the moral analysis; but Swift's book also has the complicated layering of meanings which we associate with allegory. Swift is the author and satirist who manipulates Gulliver as narrator and naive hero. The former shows how the latter's gullibility and idealism are both betrayed (not always to Gulliver's discredit) by a series of imagined worlds mirroring the actual world. In view of the astonishing nature of Gulliver's misanthropic conclusion, it is important to realize the sheer ordinariness of Gulliver's initial self-presentation. The first four paragraphs of the book are, like *Robinson Crusoe*, circumstantially realistic. Gulliver is an unexceptionable middle-class Englishman of modest means and background from the middle of England, the middle of five sons. Together

34

with his frontispiece portrait (added in the 1735 edition), the cumulative impression is of an immediately recognizable ordinariness within a conventional literary mode. The vitriolic misanthrope who screams at us at the end of the fourth voyage is the very same man who writes, in the first chapter, of himself and his fellow men in balanced and even affectionate terms. We must accept that the disintegration of Gulliver is sequential, that it happens as the events that provoke it are described, and that Gulliver's final lunacy is carefully disguised at least during the first three voyages. Even so, Swift's signals of Gulliver's crazy nature are unmistakable. The letter to Sympson ('written' in 1727 but not published until Faulkner's edition of 1735) complains mightily that the world has not been morally reformed since the first edition of Gulliver's book; the 1735 edition was to carry a portrait of Gulliver over the legend 'Splendide Mendax' (magnificent liar). Indeed, none of Swift's narrators, in *A Tale*, in the *Travels*, or in *A Modest Proposal*, is given complete autonomy. They are all given only as much psychological authenticity as will allow their manipulation by Swift for self-entrapment. Swift characteristically mocked his own seriousness; in his satires he mocked all those who pretended to authority. Every characteristic detail of Gulliver's personality – his ordinariness, his short sight, his bodily self-consciousness, his early interest in scientific schemes, his patriotism – will carry a *satiric* potential. The first voyage to the tiny country of Lilliput will confirm his European sense of superiority just as his experiences in the gigantic world of Brobdingnag will for a time diminish and intimidate him. Swift is concerned to show the relativity of all things. Even though Gulliver remains the same size throughout the travels he gets smaller both in stature and in moral confidence. In the land of the Houyhnhnms the only cognate species is the filthy anthropoid Yahoo, and Gulliver is alone. The third voyage (written last) disrupts this neat comedy of relativities by an encounter with a wide range of intellectual inanities, but even so it is clear that Swift's mind runs here and throughout the whole book on one simple but timeless dilemma: man is both a risen ape and a fallen angel, a paradox of conflicting imperatives, torn between his animal nature and his aspiring rational intellect. Alexander Pope's *An Essay on Man* (1733, Epistle II, ll. 3–18) summarized this paradoxical nature brilliantly:

> *Plac'd on this isthmus of a middle state,*
> *A being darkly wise, and rudely great:*
> *With too much knowledge for the Sceptic side,*
> *With too much weakness for the Stoic's pride,*

> *He hangs between; in doubt to act, or rest,*
> *In doubt to deem himself a God, or Beast;*
> *In doubt his Mind or Body to prefer,*
> *Born but to die, and reas'ning but to err;*
> *Alike in ignorance, his reason such,*
> *Whether he thinks too little, or too much:*
> *Chaos of Thought and Passion, all confus'd;*
> *Still by himself abus'd, or disabus'd;*
> *Created half to rise, and half to fall;*
> *Great lord of all things, yet a prey to all;*
> *Sole judge of Truth, in endless Error hurl'd:*
> *The glory, jest, and riddle of the world!*

Behind all the apparent specificity of Gulliver's autobiographical narrative there is an essay on man's nature as profoundly universal as Pope's lines, and just as comically pessimistic in its conclusion. In part I Gulliver is isolated by a shipwreck (an act of nature); in part II he is abandoned by his fellows when they sight a Brobdingnagian and run for their lives (an act of human betrayal); in part III he is captured by pirates and set adrift in a canoe (a malicious act of cruelty by a Dutchman and fellow Protestant); and in part IV, where Gulliver is now a captain, his men mutiny and set him ashore for a further period of isolation. It is as though humanity itself is refining the cruelties of nature in an incremental progress of moral degradation. Gulliver's final misanthropy seems to have *some* justification in his own experience.

The main themes of 'A Voyage to Lilliput' are measurement, dominance, imprisonment, and alienation; and here more than in any other voyage the tone is comic. Gulliver is the helpless victim of human creatures 'not six inches high' who are nevertheless mathematically adept engineers. By comparison Gulliver seems burdened by awkward and undeniable physical needs (for food, drink, and bodily evacuation). Some of the essential characteristics of his nature are already being pressed home. Chained up like a dog, Gulliver both reveals and apologizes for his necessary actions, and immediately seeks the reader's indulgence:

I had been for some Hours extremely pressed by the Necessities of Nature; which was no Wonder, it being almost two days since I had last disburthened myself. I was under great Difficulties between Urgency and Shame. The best expedient I could think on, was to creep into my House, which I accordingly did; and shutting the Gate after me, I went as far as the Length of my Chain would suffer; and

36

discharged my Body of that uneasy Load. But this was the only Time I was ever guilty of so uncleanly an Action; for which I cannot but hope the candid Reader will give some Allowance, after he hath maturely and impartially considered my Case, and the Distress I was in.   (I, 2)

Humiliation is quickly followed by a Lilliputian inventory of Gulliver's belongings, and commonplace objects such as a handkerchief, snuffbox, journal, guns, money, razor, knife, fob watch, purse, sword, bullets and gunpowder are all transformed into objects without known significance or function. In this comedy of perception it is significant that the two objects Gulliver conceals from his captors are a pair of spectacles (Gulliver is short-sighted) and a telescope, subtle hints of the visual relativities behind which Lilliputian society and the later Brobdingnagian experience are to enact in allegorical terms the absurdities of English society itself, and particularly the politics of 1708 to 1715. At the Emperor's court he attends an exhibition of rope-dancing, of '*leaping* and *creeping*' for political preferment. Cavalry manoeuvres between the legs of Gulliver the Man-Mountain turn Gulliver himself into an exhibition, and the holes in his breeches 'afforded some Opportunities for Laughter and Admiration' to the passing squadrons. Broad comedy gives way to political allegory when Gulliver learns of Lilliputian factionalism and the threat of invasion from the neighbouring Blefuscu. Under the almost identical names of Tramecksan and Slamecksan (differentiated only by their high and low heels) Swift mirrors the High Church Tory and the Low Church Whig parties. Blefuscu stands for France, with whom England had been at war from 1689 to 1697, and again, in the War of the Spanish Succession, from 1701 to 1713. The Lilliput–Blefuscu conflict had originated in a dispute as to which end of an egg to break first, and although there are a number of possible interpretations of this symbol within the obvious and broad religious dispute since the Reformation between Catholics (Big-Endians) and Anglicans (Small-Endians), it is perfectly clear that Swift's imagination is running on the *general* absurdity of religious and political tribalism. Gulliver's own opinion is that such matters as *which* religious or political loyalty to choose should be 'left to every Man's Conscience, or at least in the Power of the Chief Magistrate to determine' (I, 4). Swift similarly drew a distinction between the individual right to private liberty of conscience and the necessity for the civil power to restrain public expression of heterodox views. In chapter 5 Gulliver's enthusiasm for Lilliputian society draws him into the war with Blefuscu. He captures the enemy fleet, but then refuses to become the instrument of the Emperor's ambition to enslave a free

37

people. Again, there is here a reflection of Swift's defence of Ireland. At this point Gulliver's position is precarious, and a junta of ministers plot his destruction. The allegory here is broadly applicable to the perils of any political career, but may lie specifically in Bolingbroke's efforts to bring the war to an end in 1713, and his subsequent fall. It may be that the indecorous method by which Gulliver extinguishes the palace fire (the war) by urinating on it (the secretly negotiated peace was technically illegal) also refers to Swift's experiences with Harley and Bolingbroke; but again, neither the comedy nor the satire are in any way dependent on topical allusion. Swift's satirical imagination is fired by specific historical events, but works in broad allegorical terms. Chapter 6 takes up some conventional themes of utopian writing, whose function is to expose English defects in the law and in morality. For example, Lilliputian laws are enforced not only by penalties, but rewards; employment in government office depends more on moral probity than professional aptitude (Swift was deeply suspicious of all claims to special professional skills) and belief in divine providence is a qualification for office. Apart from the necessity to propagate the species, the family has no function in the rearing of children in Lilliput. Offspring of the upper and middle classes are educated in single-sex academies which minimize sexist discriminations. As to those we would call the lower classes, however, 'their Business being only to till and cultivate the Earth . . . their Education is of little Consequence to the Publick'. Gulliver's account of such social practices is qualified by an increasing awareness of Lilliputian imperfections, however. In theory they may once have been admirable, in practice they too have become victims of 'the most scandalous Corruptions' induced by 'the degenerate Nature of Man' (I, 6). Hunted by Skyris Bolgolam (High Admiral) and Flimnap (the High Treasurer), both presumably only six inches high, Gulliver is impeached for treasonable acts and is sentenced to blinding. He escapes to Blefuscu, but this time alert to the duplicity and ambition of princes. He returns to England and his wife, his pockets crammed with miniature cattle and sheep.

The pattern of part I is repeated in each subsequent part. The constitutionally restless Gulliver sets off on his voyages only to be isolated and imprisoned by a process of increasing human knavery, left alone as an unaccommodated wretch to survive as best he may. 'Discovered' by the strange inhabitants of undiscovered lands, he is gradually inducted into their societies, at the court of emperors, kings and leaders, and is drawn to compare what he sees with what he has known. Among the Lilliputians Gulliver initially at least associates physical inferiority with moral superiority. Among the Brobdingnagians his initial terror gives way to admiration, but in this voyage Swift begins to drive wedges between Gulliver's narrative authority and his inner confidence. Whereas in Lilliput Gulliver had been trapped by small humans, Gulliver in Brobdingnag is alienated by Nature itself: the grass is twenty feet high, corn is forty feet high, it takes him an hour to walk across a field, a hedge is a hundred and twenty feet high, and a stile is quite beyond his ability to mount. Like a mouse in a field, he is threatened with a reaping hook, and fears the inhabitants on the principle that 'human Creatures are observed to be more Savage and cruel in Proportion to their Bulk' (II, 1). He compares himself to a weasel, toad, spider, sparrow, rabbit, kitten and puppy dog. He is terrorized by cats, dogs and rats, drinks out of a thimble (in Lilliput he had been 'rationed' to the food and drink equivalent to that consumed by 1,728 citizens), is shown off like a performing monkey at country fairs, and is eventually sent for by the court. From entertaining the rabble he must now entertain the aristocracy. The King's expert scholars determine Gulliver's oddity; with no natural means of self-defence he is labelled a freak of nature. The new relativity of size means that it is Gulliver's turn to be interrogated. Instead of oblique and allegorical satire Swift uses the King's viewpoint to indulge in Olympian ridicule. Of the first interview between Gulliver and the King of Brobdingnag, Gulliver gives this account:

This Prince took a Pleasure in conversing with me; enquiring into the Manners, Religion, Laws, Government, and Learning of *Europe*, wherein I gave him the best Account I was able. His Apprehension was so clear, and his Judgment so exact, that he made very wise Reflexions and Observations upon all I said. But, I confess, that after I had been a little too copious in talking of my beloved Country; of our Trade, and Wars by Sea and Land, of our Schisms in Religion, and Parties in the State; the Prejudices of his Education prevailed so far, that he could not forbear taking me up in his right Hand, and stroaking me gently with the other; after an hearty Fit of laughing, asked me whether I were a *Whig* or a *Tory*. Then turning to his first Minister, who waited behind him with a white Staff, near as tall as the Main-mast of the Royal *Sovereign*; he observed how contemptible a Thing was human Grandeur, which could be mimicked by such diminutive Insects as I; And yet, said he, I dare engage, those Creatures have their Titles and Distinctions of Honour; they contrive little Nests and Burrows, that they call Houses and Cities; they make a Figure in Dress and Equipage; they love, they fight, they dispute, they cheat, they betray. And thus he continued on, while my Colour came and went several Times, with Indignation to hear our noble Country, the Mistress of Arts and Arms, the Scourge of *France*, the Arbitress of *Europe*, the Seat of Virtue, Piety, Honour and Truth, the Pride and Envy of the World, so contemptuously treated.   (II, 3)

39

For Swift's own gloss on the King's rueful question, there is the following passage in *The Sentiments of a Church of England Man* (1708):

This Spirit of Faction . . . [has] Broke all the Laws of Charity, Neighbourhood, Alliance, and Hospitality; destroyed all Ties of Friendship, and divided Families against themselves . . . And no Wonder it should be so, when in order to find out the Character of a Person; instead of inquiring whether he be a Man of Virtue, Honour, Piety, Wit, Good Sense, or Learning; the modern Question is only, Whether he be a *Whig* or a *Tory*.   (*Prose Works*, II, 24)

Doubtless the King of Brobdingnag is here used by Swift to show Gulliver at least out of his depth, if not actively self-deceiving. The King sees through Gulliver's encomium of European institutions, but yet is equally determined to put the *worst* interpretation possible on Gulliver's account. Gulliver reacts to penetrating criticism by asserting England to be a moral and political paradise, and the argument is illustrated in extreme terms only. Gulliver cannot cope with the King's perspicacity and compensates by inflating particular details to grotesque and repulsive proportions: the woman with a cancer in her breast, 'swelled to a monstrous Size, full of Holes, in two or three of which I could have easily crept'; the gigantic lice crawling on the Brobdingnagians' clothes. In chapter 5 his self-esteem is further assailed when his nurse Glumdalclitch carelessly abandons him in an orchard and he is knocked flat by a falling apple. He is bruised from head to foot by a hailstorm, he falls into a mole-hole, barks his shin on a snail shell, is attacked by a frog and, in an anticipation of the fourth voyage, he is kidnapped and affectionately caressed by a monkey. His sexual identity is further disturbed when he is overcome by the offensive body odour of the Maid of Honour's bosom, but it is a typical Swiftian touch for Gulliver to remark: 'those illustrious Persons were no more disagreeable to their Lovers, or to each other, than People of the same Quality are with us in *England*. And, after all, I found their natural Smell was much more supportable than when they used Perfumes, under which I immediately swooned away.' Here and elsewhere in the *Travels* we catch a glimpse of Swift's fundamental scepticism, as expressed, for example, in his letter to Pope of 26 November 1725:

I tell you after all that I do not hate mankind, it is vous autres who hate them because you would have them reasonable animals, and are angry for being disappointed. I have always rejected that definition and made another of my own. I am no more angry with [Walpole] than I was with the kite that last week flew away with one of my chickens and yet I was pleased when one of my servants shot him two days after.   (*Correspondence*, III, 118)

Or there is the comment on Gulliver's own penultimate paragraph in part IV:

> My Reconcilement to the *Yahoo*-kind in general might not be so difficult, if they would be content with those Vices and Follies only which Nature hath entitled them to.

Or Swift's advice to his friend Sheridan after the latter had committed a professionally suicidal tactical and political blunder on his first appearance in a new parish: 'expect no more from man than such an animal is capable of, and you will every day find my description of Yahoos more resembling. You should think and deal with every man as a villain, without calling him so, or flying from him, or valuing him less' (11 September 1725). If such advice seems better to describe the King rather than Gulliver, then this is a measure of Gulliver's naivety. In chapters 6 and 7 of part II Gulliver's patriotism is shown as a compound of breezy and ignorant idealism, his political awareness conditioned by desirable theoretical aims rather than moderated by first-hand experience, and he eventually buckles under the King's *moral* interpretation of English history during the seventeenth century, 'protesting it was only an Heap of Conspiracies, Rebellions, Murders, Massacres, Revolutions, Banishments; the very worst Effects that Avarice, Faction, Hypocrisy, Perfidiousness, Cruelty, Rage, Madness, Hatred, Envy, Lust, Malice, and Ambition could produce'. The driving energy of this levelling list is Swift's own. At this stage Gulliver is the protesting victim of a view of degenerate human nature which he had earlier used on the Lilliputians. At the end of part IV he will adopt the King's view of everyone but himself, but at this point he eludes personal inclusion in the King's generalization of Humanity as 'the most pernicious Race of little odious Vermin that Nature ever suffered to crawl upon the Surface of the Earth' by dismissing the King's arguments as the product of prejudice and narrow-mindedness, 'from which we and the politer Countries of *Europe* are wholly exempted'. That last manoeuvre traps Gulliver in Swift's satirical plot. Throughout these two crucial chapters morality is opposed to politics, utopian idealism to pragmatic reality, the King's detachment to Gulliver's implication as spokesman and patriotic defence counsel for his country. Swift underlines the polar oppositions by reinforcing the 'common Sense and Reason' of the Brobdingnagian system of government, their principle of utility in scientific and mechanical arts, their aversion to multiplying interpretations of the law, even their style ('clear, masculine and smooth'). Against this Gulliver can offer the King the military superiority of gunpowder, cannon balls, and thousands of books on theories of government.

On his return to England after the first two voyages Gulliver's moral perspective adjusts to normality more quickly than his visual conditioning. After each of the three voyages he returns to his unnamed wife and his two (eventually three) children, but after a few months of domesticity his Crusoe-like 'insatiable Desire of seeing foreign Countries' (I, 8), his 'evil Destiny' (II, 8), and his inability to learn 'the Lesson of knowing when I was well [off]' (IV, 1) drive him to seek fresh adventures.

ii Satire on Modern Learning: Part III

As early as 1714 Swift was looking for help in his Scriblerian satire on Modern learning. To Arbuthnot, he wrote: 'I could putt together, and lard, and strike out well enough, but all that relates to the Sciences must be from you.' Although Swift seems to have turned down Arbuthnot's help in connection with Gulliver's third voyage to Laputa, it has seemed to many readers (including Arbuthnot himself) that it sits uneasily between Brobdingnag and Houyhnhnmland. This is not simply because this imagined world is populated by real men, thus breaking the logical progression in Gulliver's physical disorientation from his own species. Swift's eye is now on intellectual folly, and size is of no concern to his argument. The comic logic of parts I, II and IV is clear, as Gulliver is progressively diminished, isolated, and also firmly under the control of Swift's intention to have him self-implicated in the satire. In part III, however, Gulliver is at times as much astonished by scientific madness as the reader, and the latter feels that Gulliver has become simply Swift's didactic mouthpiece. Having learnt to mistrust him in part II, we must now cheer his scepticism in part III. The persons, theories and activities Gulliver deplores in part III are to be deplored. Moreover, the sheer variety of situations, incidents, episodes and themes in this voyage suggests that Swift had too much material for a single vision and substituted a kaleidoscope for the single lens of Lilliput and Brobdingnag. It is usually said that Swift attacks only the gross absurdities in contemporary science, but this is not the full story. Neither is it sufficient to explain away the anti-scientific satire by reference to a satirical tradition of such writing, in Rabelais' *Gargantua and Pantagruel* or in Shadwell's *The Virtuoso* (1676), for example. The language of Swift's satire reveals a reductive and radical offence at certain intellectual activities, his metaphors often excremental or cruel, the comedy broad and at times farcical.

In Defoe's *Robinson Crusoe* the single most dramatic incident, and one of the most astonishing in all fiction, is his sudden discovery of a single footprint on an island previously thought to be uninhabited. In *Gulliver's Travels* it is only a matter of time before Gulliver's isolation is ended by contact with a whole alien society. In the third voyage his first experience is with a technological phenomenon: the Laputian Flying Island, an unidentified but populated U F O. The attributes and characteristics of the Laputians are astronomical, musical and mathematical, signs of their disembodied intellectual obsession and of their indifference to all practicality. The Laputians attempt to make real and concrete their perception of abstract harmonies, and Gulliver's first meal with them is 'a Shoulder of Mutton, cut into an Aequilateral Triangle; a Piece of Beef into a Rhomboides; and a Pudding into a Cycloid . . . two Ducks, trussed up into the Form of Fiddles . . . the Servants cut our Bread into Cones, Cylinders, Parallelograms, and several other Mathematical Figures'. Just as the sect who worship the tailor-god in *A Tale of a Tub* substitute the outside for the inside, so the Laputians have sublimated the complexities of actual living into the elegant theorems of number and geometry. They are the perversely extreme example of one of Swift's own maxims, that 'wherever God hath left to man the power of interposing a remedy for thought or labour, there he hath placed things in a state of imperfection, on purpose to stir up human industry, without which life would stagnate, or indeed could not rather subsist at all' (*Thoughts on Various Subjects, Prose Works*, IV, 245). As aristocrats of the intellect they scorn the arts of the mechanic; hyperdevelopment of their abstract and theoretical skills make them instant experts on social politics, yet their astronomical prediction of planetary collision denies them a good night's sleep, while their wives and daughters pass their time in unsupervised promiscuity (a domestic separation of the intellectual and physical imperatives).

Behind the specific and pseudo-scientific description of the Flying Island's logistics there is an account of England's attempted domination of the Irish economy through the imposition of something as mundane as the minting of copper coin. The last five paragraphs of chapter 3 (from 'About three Years before my Arrival' to 'change the Government') were suppressed in both Motte's and Faulkner's two editions of the *Travels* printed in 1726, 1735 and 1738. The paragraphs existed in Charles Ford's interleaved copy of the first edition and were not published until 1896. Briefly, William Wood was given a patent by the English government to supply Ireland with copper coins to the value of £108,000 in 1722, helped by a large bribe to the Duchess of Kendal. Swift's campaign against Wood and the scheme itself, conducted in *The*

Drapier's Letters, obliged Walpole's government to withdraw the scheme altogether in the autumn of 1725, and the episode is here transformed into a rebellion of the Lindalinians (the Dublin Irish) against Laputian (English) tyranny, with this final comment from the victorious Swift: 'I was assured by a great Minister, that if the Island had descended so near the Town, as not to be able to raise it self, the Citizens were determined to fix it for ever, to kill the King and all his Servants, and entirely change the Government.'

In chapters 4 to 6 Gulliver is in the metropolis of Lagado, a city of desolation and decay, but with one notable and precarious exception. Lord Munodi's estate, 'built according to the best Rules of ancient Architecture', is a symbol of perfection threatened by the modish obsession for mathematical regularity propagated by the Academy of Projectors. There are perhaps elements of Temple and Bolingbroke in Munodi, each of whom disdained the world's craziness for an ideal of retirement. Tactically, Swift is exposing Gulliver to an image of tradi-tional aristocratic culture before submerging him in the lunacies of 'Modern' mechanistic science. Of the fourteen projects in chapter 5, several are recognizable derivations from actual experiments published in the *Transactions of the Royal Society*. Many of these were included in a three-volume collection produced by Edmund Halley and William Derham in 1705–7, entitled *Miscellanea Curiosa*. Gulliver points out that the Academy of Lagado had been established 'about Forty Years ago' (i.e. in 1667, if Gulliver is recounting his experiences in 1707/8). The Royal Society received its first charter in 1662. In the first number of the *Transactions* (6 March 1665) there were the following articles:

An Accompt of the improvement of Optick Glasses at Rome. Of the Observation made in England of a Spot in one of the Belts of the Planet Jupiter. Of the Motion of the late Comet predicted. The heads of many new Observations and Experi-ments, in order to an Experimental History of Cold, together with some ther-mometrical discourses and experiments. A relation of a very odd monstrous Calf ... A Narrative concerning the success of the pendulum watches at sea for the longitudes; and the grant of a Patent thereupon ...

Swift chose to isolate the oddities and ignore the possibility of a revolution in human knowledge. If some of the experiments seemed daft, others were to affect the course of human history in the profoundest possible ways. The astronomer Flamsteed was a member of the Royal Society, as was Halley (in 1678), and Sir Isaac Newton. The Society had published such seminal works as Robert Hooke's *Micrographia or Some*

Physiological Descriptions of Minute Bodies Made by Magnifying Glasses
(1665), and Newton's paper on movement (1686), out of which grew his
Principia (1687), and also Bishop Sprat's *History of the Royal Society of
London* (1667), a third of which is devoted to justifying theoretical and
applied scientific research. One of its linguistic enunciations anti~inated
the Lagadian scheme for reducing language to things, 'by
Polysyllables into one, and leaving out Verbs and Participles; b
Reality all things imaginable are but Nouns'. Sprat writes that
Society operates 'a constant Resolution, to reject all the amp
digressions, and swellings of style: to return back to the primi
and shortness, when men deliver'd so many *things*, almost
number of *words* ... bringing all things as near the N
plainness, as they can: and preferring the language
Countrymen, and Merchants, before that, of Wits, or Sch
delicious social irony, the Lagadian scheme is sabotage
those groups to whom Sprat had looked for a denot
Women ... the Vulgar and Illiterate ... Such constant .. ....cable
Enemies to Science are the common People' (III, 5).

Sprat, one of three bishops in the Royal Society (not to mention five
doctors of divinity in a total of ninety-five Fellows), argued for the
'innocence' of experimental science and its compatibility with orthodox
religious belief. Although Swift does not overtly attack the projectors on
religious grounds, he nevertheless rejects the argument of 'innocence'
and additionally parodies their efforts in language heavy with moral
disapprobation. Miracles of improbability are to be achieved with very
little effort; elegant mechanical theories will solve, at a stroke, complex
intellectual problems; the tedium of learning and close study will be
replaced by quick and easy methods available to all, irrespective of
intelligence.

Swift's catalogue of scientific inanities is only apparently miscel-
laneous. All are connected by a perverse attempt to combine natural
opposites and to discover transformations of the mundane or irksome
into the useful and luxurious. To this extent, Swift's sub-theme is the
ancient delusion that base metals can be turned into gold: his imagination
plays with the extremities of intellectual aspiration out of touch with
physical realities, the signs of which are bodily unpleasantness. The
projectors themselves are not only deranged in the sense that their minds
have abandoned their bodies, they are also dirty, smelly and unintelligible. Cucumbers may be turned into sunbeams, excrement may be re-
cycled into its original constituents, ice may be turned into gunpowder, a
blind man may be taught how to identify colours, hogs may be used to

plough the fields by systematically burying their food, cobwebs may be made into silk, marble may be softened to make pincushions, and a machine has been constructed for writing books on philosophy, poetry, politics, law, mathematics and theology – all without the least intellectual qualification. Almost every scheme attempts to deny the natural and unavoidable barriers to human effort and the inevitabilities of natural processes. As an emblem of them all, the project to abandon words altogether and to substitute *things* for *words* suggests that Swift's deepest objection to experimental science is its obsession with the *physical* world at the expense of *moral* philosophy. Some members of the Royal Academy had written papers on the analogies between the two most abstract arts, music and mathematics (the Royal Academy of Music had been established in 1719), and Swift highlights this extreme form of abstract speculation as an evasion of man's primarily moral duties.

Gulliver's account of the scientists in Lagado is detached and impartial, not only because 'I had my self been a Sort of Projector in my younger Days' (III, 4), but also because additional satirical underlining of such gross absurdities would be strategically superfluous. But in chapter 6 Gulliver does not hesitate to evaluate the School of political Projectors as 'wholly out of their Senses'. Their attempts to match political preferment with a programme of moral virtue are dismissed as 'wild impossible Chimaeras'. Of the least lunatic, Gulliver selects those who would see an entirely physical cause for the proliferation of abstract political theories. Lagadian surgeons operate on the body politic, arguing that social faction is a disease of the individual brain:

When Parties in a State are violent, he offered a wonderful Contrivance to reconcile them. The Method is this. You take an Hundred Leaders of each Party; you dispose them into Couples of such whose Heads are nearest of a Size; then let two nice Operators saw off the *Occiput* of each Couple at the same Time, in such a Manner that the Brain may be equally divided. Let the *Occiputs* thus cut off be interchanged, applying each to the Head of his opposite Party-Man. It seems indeed to be a Work that requireth some Exactness; but the Professor assured us, that if it were dextrously performed, the Cure would be infallible. For he argued thus; that the two half Brains being left to debate the Matter between themselves within the Space of one Scull, would soon come to a good Understanding, and produce that Moderation as well as Regularity of Thinking, so much to be wished for in the Heads of those, who imagine they came into the World only to watch and govern its Motion: And as to the Difference of Brains in Quantity or Quality, among those who are Directors in Faction; the Doctor assured us from his own Knowledge, that it was a perfect Trifle.

This ludicrously mechanical solution to an intellectual problem both ridicules those who suffer from its symptoms and deepens the dismay of those who have watched its social effects. The passage ends with a fine and dismissive irony which of course dehumanizes political leaders and at the same time suggests that in their professional life they are externalizing their own schizophrenia. In his discussion with the Laputian political theorists Gulliver's discoveries overlap with Swift's experience: the cryptographers described in the last three paragraphs of chapter 6 reflect in quite precise terms the ciphers used in evidence to convict Bishop Atterbury in 1723. As if to underline the uncomfortable parallel, Gulliver's attention turns to home.

Swift clearly regarded man's prime duty as moral self-knowledge. In any contest between moral philosophy and natural philosophy (or 'science'), the former takes precedence. As Pope was to put it, 'The proper Study of Mankind is Man', and as Johnson stated in his *Life of Milton*, 'we are perpetually moralists, but we are geometricians only by chance . . . Physical knowledge is of such rare emergence, that one man may know another half his life without being able to estimate his skill in hydrostaticks or astronomy; but his moral and prudential character immediately appears.'

For Swift the great unresolved questions about man's nature far exceeded the possible benefits from speculative and experimental science. Swift also seems to have seen the two activities as mutually exclusive, as a dichotomy within the intellectual powers. At its most extreme, the unresolved and unresolvable tension between the intellectual and the animal in man's nature (again, an unrealistic dichotomy since man *is* an animal) is suddenly and urgently resurrected in Glubbdubdrib and Luggnagg (chapters 7 to 10). Released from the tyranny of historical time, Gulliver is entertained by a pageant which includes Hannibal, Caesar, Pompey, Brutus, Socrates, the Theban general Epaminondas, Cato the Stoic, and Sir Thomas More (author of the most important single influence on *Gulliver's Travels*). In comparing the Senate of Rome with its 'modern Representative', Gulliver remarks: 'The first seemed to be an Assembly of Heroes and Demy-Gods; the other a Knot of Pedlars, Pick-pockets, Highwaymen and Bullies.' Gulliver, like his creator, is particularly attracted to those historical figures who destroy tyrants and defend liberties, implying both their need and their absence in the contemporary world. In a further interview, he observes that neither Homer nor Aristotle recognize any of their commentators: Moderns come off badly, and Aristotle finds both Peter Ramus and Descartes unintelligible. Throughout this section the conviction of history as a process of decline and misinterpretation gathers force. Intellectual ignorance increases due to a lust for speculative knowledge, and a genetic debasement of the human race goes hand in hand with its moral dissolution, only to become the badge of social preference: 'How Cruelty, Falshood, and Cowardice grew to be Characteristics by which certain Families are distinguished as much by their Coat of Arms. Who first brought the *Pox* into a noble House, which hath lineally descended in scrophulous Tumours to their Posterity. Neither could I wonder at all this, when I saw such an Interruption of Lineages by Pages, Lacqueys, Valets, Coachmen, Gamesters, Fidlers, Players, Captains, and Pick-pockets.' In spite of his lowly origins, Gulliver expresses a horror at the contamination of aristocratic bloodstock by servants, entertainers and criminals which immediately becomes a theoretical framework and a justification for an interpretation of his own present. He now believes that history is explicable by a theory of conspiracy. Gulliver's disclaimer, that what he says is not to be applied to his own country, is Swift's irony at its elbow-nudging simplest. Gulliver's pronouncements on degeneration are in fact sweepingly applied to 'the Race of human Kind ... within these Hundred Years past'. Such sweeping pessimism is but one step from the abject moral horror at humanity expressed in the final voyage. Under the spreading tree of Gulliver's ego only pigmies will be seen to grow from now on.

Swift always goes much further than we might either expect or fear, and although the desire for immortal life may be a commonplace in travellers' tales (Pliny's *Natural History*), in parodic travellers' tales (Lucian's *True History*), in classical satire (Juvenal's *Satire* X), in mythology (Tithonus), and in the rewards of religious belief, nothing so far quite prepares us for the visceral nastiness of the Struldbruggs, an elite cadre of beings condemned to everlasting life *without* everlasting youth. As Swift remarked in one of his maxims, 'Every man desires to live long; but no man would be old.' Swift's eye is not focused on the inevitable humiliations of old age as such, but on the horror of life continuing as the physical and intellectual powers diminish. Beyond eighty years the Struldbruggs are legally regarded as dead; they are indifferent to human friendship and affection, racked by envy and impotence, and amnesiac. They outlive their own generation and its language, to survive as hated objects, aliens in a hostile world. Yet throughout this section there *is* a sense of Swift's own terror of old age, a premonition, as it were, of his own end not only as an individual but also as a Christian. It is characteristic of *Gulliver's Travels* that spiritual anguish is largely absent from this *memento mori*: the worst penalties of old age are human isolation and physical ugliness, not spiritual despair, and it is as though continuity of life means no more than an intensification of man's innate moral and physical corruption. Like T. S. Eliot's Gerontion, nothing lives in their memory, and Gulliver further remarks, 'They were the most horrifying Sight I ever beheld; and the Women more horrible than the Men.' As a sermon on the foolishness of fearing death, this chapter also shows what makes life worth living. If we reverse the list of Struldbrugg vices, we can infer the positive qualities of toleration, generosity, humour, self-control, social affection, and above all friendship, without which life is in any terms intolerable. When Swift himself wrote down a list of maxims in 1699 (at the age of thirty-two!) entitled 'When I come to be old' he listed precisely those characteristics later to be negatively exemplified in the Struldbruggs: 'Not to be peevish, or morose, or suspicious . . . Not to be covetous . . . Not to neglect decency, or cleanliness, for fear of falling into nastiness . . . Not to be over severe with young people, but give allowances for their youthful follies and weaknesses . . . Not to talk much, nor of myself', and so on. Swift also added a final maxim, 'Not to set up for observing all these rules, for fear I should observe none.'

The third part of *Gulliver's Travels* was written after the composition of part IV. They are nevertheless thematically sequential in their final ordering. The predominantly *intellectual* satire of part III ends with an image of grotesque *physical* decay, providing a logical and a thematic progression towards the climactic voyage to the Houyhnhnms, the longest and the most complex episode of the whole book.

iii 'The Beast and I': Part IV and the Nature of Man

The next great Attack . . . is not less then upon a *British* Parliament; this august Assembly, the Wisest, the Noblest, the most Awful in the World, he treats with Words of the utmost Scurrility, with *Billingsgate* terms of the lowest Sort; this Body of the best Gentlemen in the Kingdom he calls Pedlars, Pickpockets, Highwaymen and Bullies; Words never spoke of a British Parliament before, and 'twould be a National Reproach they should now pass unpunished: This is beyond all Bounds; who that are *English* Men can with Temper think of such an Insult upon the Body of their Representatives; the Centre of the National Power; the great Preserver of our Laws, Religion, and Liberties, and of all that as Men and Christians we ought to hold dear and valuable.

Anonymous *Letter from a Clergyman to his Friend*
(1726), on *Gulliver's Travels*

I meddle not the least with any *Party*, but write without Passion, Prejudice, or Ill-will against any Man or Number of Men whatsoever. I write for the noblest

End, to inform and instruct Mankind, over whom I may, without Breach of Modesty, pretend to some Superiority, from the Advantages I received by conversing so long among the most accomplished *Houyhnhnms.* I write without any View towards Profit or Praise. I never suffer a Word to pass that may look like Reflection, or possibly give the least Offence even to those who are most ready to take it. So that, I hope, I may with Justice pronounce myself an Author perfectly blameless; against whom the Tribes of Answerers, Considerers, Observers, Reflecters, Detecters, Remarkers, will never be able to find Matter for exercising their Talent.

Gulliver's Travels, IV, 12

As for the humour and conduct of this famous fable, I suppose there is no person who reads but must admire; as for the moral, I think it is horrible, shameful, unmanly, blasphemous ... When Gulliver first lands among the Yahoos, the naked howling wretches clamber up trees and assault him, and he describes himself as 'almost stifled with the filth which fell about him'. The reader of the fourth part of *Gulliver's Travels* is like the hero himself in this instance. It is Yahoo language: a monster gibbering shrieks, and gnashing imprecations against mankind – tearing down all shreds of modesty, past all sense of manliness and shame; filthy in word, filthy in thought, furious, raging, obscene ... the meaning is that man is utterly wicked, desperate, and imbecile, and his passions are so monstrous, and his boasted powers so mean, that he is and deserves to be the slave of brutes, and ignorance is better than his vaunted reason. What had this man done? what secret remorse was rankling at his heart? what fever was boiling in him, that he should see all the world blood-shot?

W. M. Thackeray, *The English Humourists* (1853)

It was an essential part of Swift's intentions to *vex* his readers. We may be tempted to dismiss Thackeray's unanswerable questions as obtuse, as hysterical as the 'meaning' he imputes to the *Travels* as a whole; but from the very beginning, the history of critical responses to the fourth voyage has vindicated Swift's expressed intention. It is impossible not to be puzzled, at the very least, by the implications and by the imagery of Gulliver's final and climactic voyage to the land of speaking rational horses and inarticulate bestial Yahoos. Such is the vividness of Swift's presentation of the Yahoo that the word itself has passed into the language as a term for all that is contemptible and anarchic in the human personality. Often discussed alone, the fourth voyage is nevertheless an integral part of the overall strategy. Its relationship with the previous voyages is a matter of increased intensity, emotional concentration, and generic moral focus. Just as Pope's first three books of the *Dunciad* are followed by a much broader satire on the institutions and social processes of dulness (as opposed to the listing of individual dunces), so Gulliver's fourth voyage takes a more radical look at the source of all the previous human inadequacies and error, human nature itself, or rather, a particular assumption that human nature is defined by its rationality. All discussions of the fourth voyage must acknowledge Swift's comments to Pope in a letter sent one month before the *Travels* was published, on 29 September 1725:

I have ever hated all Nations professions and Communityes and all my love is towards individualls, for instance I hate the tribe of Lawyers, but I love Councellor such a one, Judge such a one for so with Physicians (I will not Speak of my own Trade) Soldiers, English, Scotch, French; and the rest but principally I hate and detest that animal called man, although I hartily love John, Peter, Thomas and so forth. This is the system upon which I have governed my self many years (but do not tell) and so I shall go on till I have done with them. I have got Materials Towards a Treatis proving the falsity of that Definition *animal rationale*; and to show it should be only *rationis capax*.* Upon this great foundation of Misanthropy (though not Timons manner) the whole Building of my Travells is erected: And I never will have peace of mind till all honest Men are of my Opinion.   (*Correspondence*, III, 103)

However schematic and overstated the conditions of Swift's love and hatred may be, there is at least on one point a clear distinction to be made between Swift's and Gulliver's viewpoint: at the end of the fourth voyage Gulliver hates *every* human being. As a character, Gulliver's experiences are of course *real* – he has actually met and conversed with rational horses – but as an instrument in a satirical argument he seems at the end of the *Travels* to be no more than the mouthpiece for a view of human nature which is pathological in its hatred. Put bluntly, the question is whether Gulliver's actions are those of either a madman or a fool. Having experienced the rational utopia of Houyhnhnms he finds return to the fallen world of man insufferable, and within the terms of an *abstract* argument this seems to be a perfectly tenable position. Having glimpsed Paradise, he must return to Hell on earth. If this is accepted, then Gulliver can hardly be mad in denouncing humanity. On the other hand, and in terms of psychological probability, his attempt to renounce his humanity by acting like (and sleeping with) a horse is nothing but certifiable lunacy, a grotesque attempt to deny half of his nature. An additional complication is that however abstract the terms of Swift's discussion of the moral nature of man might be, it is the astonishing specificity of the Yahoos in particular that carries with it deep and perhaps not altogether conscious loathings based not only upon traditional (and specifically Christian) images of sin but on Swift's own free imagination. It is characteristic of Swift to leave paradoxes unresolved,

* i.e. *capable* of rationality, but not by definition rational.

to deny the logical solution, to widen the difficulties of interpretation rather than narrow them by a stroke of authorial intervention, and to undercut the certainties of a conclusion by ironic means. All these things happen in the fourth voyage.

As in all the other voyages, part IV begins with the familiar certainties of circumstantial realism before moving off into a substitute world. Gulliver is no longer a surgeon but a captain; his men mutiny and set him ashore alone. Gulliver spends less time narrating the metamorphosis of his surroundings than in any previous voyage. His first meeting with the Yahoos, though disagreeable to his instincts, is incidental to his purpose of discovering human presence. The group of Yahoos who attack him are frightened off by the arrival of a horse, and Gulliver begins to interpret equine gestures anthropomorphically, being 'so orderly and rational, so acute and judicious', the more so by contrast with the filthy Yahoos. Their language, however, 'expressed the Passions very well' (feelings and emotions rather than rational concepts), an indication that these creatures are not rational machines but truly *natural* creatures. At this point Gulliver attributes this equine intellectual grace to human training, but such speculations are cut short when the Master Horse and Sorrel Nag put Gulliver side by side with a Yahoo. Gulliver's reaction is one of the destabilizing high points of the whole book:

The Beast and I were brought close together; and our Countenances diligently compared, both by Master and Servant, who thereupon repeated several Times the Word *Yahoo*. My Horror and Astonishment are not to be described, when I observed, in this abominable Animal, a perfect human Figure . . .

Unable to eat the food he is offered, he remarks:

I now apprehended, that I must absolutely starve, if I did not get to some of my own Species: For as to those filthy *Yahoos*, although there were few greater Lovers of Mankind, at that time, than myself; yet I confess I never saw any sensitive Being so detestable on all Accounts; and the more I came near them, the more hateful they grew, while I stayed in that Country.   (IV, 2)

Gulliver's eventual lunacy starts at this point, where he *identifies* the Yahoo with 'Mankind'. Thackeray's comment quoted above also indicates that some of Swift's readers have chosen to draw the same equation as Gulliver, and have assumed that what Gulliver says is what Swift himself believes. What has happened, we might suggest, is that the anthropological specificity of Gulliver's description of the Yahoos unleashes deeper memories of the Yahoos as a *symbol* of human depravity.

The Yahoos are certainly disgusting, but they are just as certainly not human, and Gulliver's error is in mistaking some casual similarities in the Yahoos for the essential characteristics of man at his moral worst. This was an error outlined by Aristotle in his *Categories* (Book III, 2, 117b) and frequently repeated with the same examples in countless elementary books on logic throughout Swift's own period:

Look also to see whether the resemblance be that of a caricature, like the resemblance of a monkey to a man, whereas a horse bears none: for the monkey is not the more handsome creature despite its nearer resemblance to man. Again, in the case of two things, if one is more like the better thing while another is more like the worse, then that is likely to be better which is more like the better ... if Man be better than Horse, then also the best Man is better than the best horse. Also, if the best in A be better than the best in B, then also A is better than B without qualification; e.g. if the best man be better than the best horse, then also Man is better than Horse without qualification.

Although this textbook example of clear thinking indicates the error of Gulliver's perception, it does not 'explain' Gulliver's decision hereafter to identify the human with the Yahoo. The decision to do so wells up from his instincts and emotions, not chiefly from his rational mind. The psychological immediacy of Gulliver's experience submerges the intellectual error in a radical change of personality, in which everything vile is associated with the Yahoo and everything admirable belongs to the Houyhnhnms. Gulliver has to choose between the two extremes, and in choosing to affiliate himself with the Houyhnhnms he pursues a higher rational ideal at the cost of his human nature. In another context Swift remarked, 'The stoical scheme of supplying our wants by lopping off our desires, is like cutting off our feet, when we want shoes.' Gulliver dispenses with his unregenerate humanity as easily as he dispenses with salt on his food.

Our view of Gulliver is increasingly dominated by the Houyhnhnms, who are astonished 'that a brute Animal should discover such Marks of a rational Creature' (IV, 3); he is different from the Yahoo only in so far as he is teachable, civil and clean. As insular as the King of Brobdingnag, the Houyhnhnms have awarded themselves racial supremacy; their name means 'the Perfection of Nature'. For as long as Gulliver keeps his body covered with clothes (which are regarded by the Houyhnhnms as part of his essential being), he is tolerated. When these are removed, the Yahoo category fits him almost perfectly, and Gulliver's characteristic if occasional bodily self-consciousness now becomes a matter of deep shame. Adam and Eve were only ashamed of their bodies after disobeying God in Eden: in Gulliver's postlapsarian world he apologizes for his physique to a horse. Again, Swift's satirical imagination works on the level of several simultaneous but not precisely analogous allegorical transferences. In Europe human beings manage brutes, in Houyhnhnmland animals manage the anthropoid Yahoos. In Europe the leaders make manifest their power and superiority by oppressing members of their own species (and using horses as beasts of burden). In Houyhnhnmland there is an absolute division of power *between* two species, most clearly manifested every fourth year, when the Houyhnhnms debate the same question, 'Whether the *Yahoos* should be exterminated from the Face of the Earth' (IV, 9). In the former there is endless wrangling, feuding, dissension, controversy and power-mongering; in the latter there is civil and intellectual harmony established by a totalitarian oligarchy based on genocidal power. At some deep level in his imagination Swift may also be drawing an analogy between English political tyranny over the Irish, and also toying with a visionary utopianism in which truths are all self-evident. The difficulty here is that part IV is quite overtly above narrow concerns for a particular race, society, or particular set of historical circumstances: Gulliver discourses with the Master Horse not merely about England but about the 'Nature of Manhood'. Swift similarly informed the Abbé Desfontaines, the French translator of the *Travels*: 'If the volumes of Gulliver were designed only for the British Isles, that traveler ought to pass for a very contemptible writer. The same vices and the same follies reign everywhere; at least in the civilized countries of Europe: and the author who writes only for one city, one province, one kingdom, or even one age, does not deserve to be read, let alone translated.' In part IV Gulliver is no longer the representative Englishman but the representative human being. Certainly, he will speak in general terms about English political institutions, prime ministers, courts, armies, etc., but under Houyhnhnm tutelage and the constraints of their simpler vocabulary, he looks at humanity with the objectivity of a zoologist or animal behaviourist. The language of the satirist becomes his natural means of expression. There are no words for 'Power, Government, War, Law, Punishment, and a Thousand other Things' in the Houyhnhnm language (IV, 4), yet Gulliver describes English as 'barbarous' (IV, 5).

Gulliver's account of European institutions and political history is 'simplified' to the point of a reductive parody of reality, in which it is impossible to discriminate between Swift's comic satire on European manners, Gulliver's asinine patriotism, blind to its own contradictions, and Swift's presumed intention to shock the reader out of his comfortable Eurocentric complacency

Poor Nations are *hungry*, and *rich* Nations are *proud*; and Pride and Hunger will ever be at Variance. For these Reasons, the Trade of a Soldier is held the most honourable of all others: Because a *Soldier* is a *Yahoo* hired to kill in cold Blood as many of his own Species, who have never offended him, as possibly he can.

(IV, 5)

Tactically, Gulliver is being absorbed into his creator's strategy and the zeal of one fuels the purposes of the other; Gulliver's experiences will show that humanity is not only corrupt (news to Gulliver, if not to Swift), but that its modicum of rationality is used to *exacerbate* natural corruption, not to conquer it. The parallel between Gulliver's final paragraph (IV, 12) and the Master Horse's conclusion in IV, 5 is striking: 'instead of Reason, we were only possessed of some Quality fitted to increase our natural Vices'. That quality, as Gulliver will point out at the end of the book, is Pride, and in revealing the ubiquity of Pride Swift and Gulliver compete with each other.

As Swift had indicated in his letter to Pope of 29 September 1725, particular animus is directed against groups of professionals: lawyers, physicians, and the military. The first group lies for pay, the second group conceals its incompetence by mechanical theories and mysterious terms, and the third makes killing a trade. Worse than any of these is 'a *First* or *Chief Minister* of *State*' (IV, 6), a paragon of vice above all others in deceit. Gulliver's description of court politics cannot be based on anything but hearsay, but from Swift this passage is clearly a scathing attack on Sir Robert Walpole and his manipulation of placemen and patronage in order to retain power. Gulliver's earlier patrician loyalties now crumble when he portrays the English nobility corrupted by venal marriages: 'a weak diseased Body, a meager Countenance, and sallow Complexion, are the true Marks of *Noble Blood*; and a healthy robust Appearance is so disgraceful in a Man of Quality, that the World concludes his real Father to have been a Groom or a Coachman'. In manipulating social and moral paradoxes, Gulliver speaks for Swift.

In less than a year's residence with the Houyhnhnms Gulliver has resolved never to return to his own kind. Up to chapter 7 it is Gulliver who tells the Master Horse about man; from here on the narrative is dominated by the Master Horse telling Gulliver about the Yahoos in circumstantial language modelled on the human situation. Gulliver, a good pupil, simply repeats the lessons he is taught as axiomatic

55

revelations. The reader is presented with clichés and commonplaces in the guise of deep truths. For example, Gulliver's Master tells him that '*Reason* alone is sufficient to govern a *Rational* Creature'. This elliptical pronouncement begs the fundamental question raised in Swift's letter to Pope, in which Swift replaces the definition of man as a rational animal by a definition which allows the *capacity* for reason. The difference is crucial. We only need to remember the comment in 'A Digression on Madness': '*Reason* [is] a very light Rider, and easily shook off', or that additional remark addressed to Pope: 'I tell you after all that I do not hate mankind, it is vous autres who hate them because you would have them reasonable animals, and are angry for being disappointed. I have always rejected that definition and made another of my own.'

In upholding a desirable ideal, Swift laughs at our inability to attain it. As Gulliver naturally responds to the laudable Houyhnhnm principles of friendship, benevolence, virtue and truth, Swift lets his humanity slip away. We aspire to the best, but we are undone by our fallen nature. That is the paradox of human nature. Idealism and a humiliating comic bathos are not alternatives, they are permanent attributes of life as lived: thus the philosopher at the end of *The Mechanical Operation of the Spirit*, one of Swift's central satirical paradigms (notwithstanding its occurrence in Plato, Cicero, Horace and Montaigne), 'who, while his Thoughts and Eyes were fixed upon the *Constellations*, found himself seduced by his *lower Parts* into a *Ditch*'. In his poems, Swift charges his idealistic lovers with the same fault: Strephon thinks of Chloe as a Goddess, and is stunned to discover that she too has bodily functions which destroy the romantic illusion. Conversely, but just as brutal in its collision of extremes, the prostitute in *A Beautiful Young Nymph Going to Bed* painfully reconstructs her ravaged body in order to deceive her clients with the superficial appearance of comeliness:

> *The Nymph, though in this mangled Plight,*
> *Must ev'ry Morn her Limbs unite.*
> *But how shall I describe her Arts*
> *To recollect her scatter'd Parts?*
> *Or show the Anguish, Toil, and Pain,*
> *Of gath'ring up herself again?*
> *The bashful Muse will never bear*
> *In such a Scene to interfere.*
> Corinna *in the morning dizen'd,*
> *Who sees, will spew; who smells, be poison'd.*
>
> (*Poems*, II, 583)

It is as though only *artifice* stands between us and the Yahoo, only social convention between human society and the abyss of avarice, ignorance, lust, sloth, and physical nastiness. Not even the Yahoos are subject to what Gulliver primly terms 'those unnatural Appetites in both Sexes, so common among us'. Gulliver makes one final experiment, an attempt to resist his Master's identification of Man and Yahoo (IV, 8), but near-rape by an eleven-year-old female Yahoo destroys whatever is left of Gulliver's human *difference*: 'For now I could no longer deny, that I was a real *Yahoo*, in every Limb and Feature, since the Females had a natural Propensity to me as one of their own Species.' The disparity in ages between Gulliver and the female Yahoo seems unnecessarily perverse, particularly when we recall that Vanessa was twenty-five years Swift's junior and Esther Johnson eight years old when Swift met her at twenty-two. One hopes that Swift intended no autobiographical parallel.

The problem with Houyhnhnm moral philosophy is that it is categorical. Directly opposed to Swift's own stated preference for individuals rather than groups, the Houyhnhnms treat only each other with 'universal' friendship and benevolence. Like Pope's Belinda in *The Rape of the Lock*, the admiration of all means the avoidance of love towards anyone in particular. In the Houyhnhnms' case this emotional frigidity extends to their own families, familial affection being regarded as irrational if it applies only to their own progeny and not to others. Eugenics is the principal ethical purpose of marriage (at least as far as the superior class is concerned, since the inferior class of servant-Houyhnhnms is allowed triple the breeding rate). Without the unremittingly statistical inhumanity of *A Modest Proposal*, the Houyhnhnm social system is nevertheless similarly grounded in a totalitarian concern for the preservation of a master race at the expense of individual freedom. Gulliver is talking about horses, but there is only a hair's breadth between his approbation of the Houyhnhnms' *rational* social practices and the black horror of the Modest Proposer's *rationalization* of England's exploitation of the subjected Ireland. The practice of animal husbandry on human beings in order to improve the quality of luxury eating is, in the case of the Houyhnhnms, replaced by an anthropomorphic description of a soulless coupling for the sake of racial improvement:

When the Matron *Houyhnhnms* have produced one of each Sex, they no longer accompany with their Consorts, except they lose one of their Issue by some Casualty, which very seldom happens: But in such a Case they meet again; or when the like Accident befalls a Person, whose Wife is past bearing, some other Couple bestows on him one of their own Colts, and then go together a second

Time, until the Mother be pregnant. This caution is necessary to prevent the Country from being over-burthened with Numbers. But the Race of inferior *Houyhnhnms* bred up to be Servants is not so strictly limited upon this Article; these are allowed to produce three of each Sex, to be Domesticks in the Noble Families.

In their Marriages they are exactly careful to chuse such Colours as will not make any disagreeable Mixture in the Breed. *Strength* is chiefly valued in the Male, and *Comeliness* in the Female; not upon the Account of *Love*, but to preserve the Race from degenerating. (IV, 8)

The common feature of this passage and *A Modest Proposal* is that both are offered to the reader as workable improvements on the current and chaotic human conventions: the busy mind can always improve on wasteful nature, it seems. In *A Modest Proposal* a worthy aim (making 'children sound and useful members of the commonwealth') entails horrific methods; in Houyhnhnmland the system of racial eugenics works only because troublesome *human* imperatives like *love* have been eradicated. Gulliver twists the knife by including that one word in a list of stratagems merely contractual in nature: 'Courtship, Love, Presents, Joyntures, Settlements have not place in their Thoughts; or Terms whereby to express them in their Language.' The evil in both proposals is the habit of mind which categorizes groups, races, sects and beliefs as instruments of others' purposes. Johnson remarked that patriotism was the last refuge of a scoundrel. Swift might have added that idealism is the *only* resort of a fool.

In a curious redaction of the creation myth, chapter 9 outlines the Houyhnhnm theory that the degenerate Yahoos post-dated their own civilization and had engendered from primordial slime. They are denied the anthropological dignity of aboriginal status, and the Houyhnhnms thereby escape the guilt of colonial exploitation. A counter-theory asserts that a male and a female had been abandoned (like Gulliver!) by their overseas companions and had since multiplied and degenerated. The Master Horse, who proposes this latter explanation, produces Gulliver in proof of it, thus explaining the marginal superiority of Gulliver to the otherwise identical Yahoo. Treading hard on the heels of the Modest Proposer, Gulliver suggests a final solution to the Yahoo problem: they should not be exterminated, but the younger Yahoos should be castrated, while the more valuable species of ass is to be cultivated, 'to be fit for Service at five Years old, which the others are not till Twelve'. In the subsequent chapter, in another parallel with *A Modest Proposal*, Gulliver signifies his distance from the Yahoo by using their skins for shoeleather.

In the midst of Gulliver's settled economy and harmony of mind as a proto-Houyhnhnm occurs one of the most extraordinary of paragraphs, in which the levelling syntax of a list reduces all moral discrimination to a stunning irrelevance. Swift's lists are a characteristic feature of his ability to juxtapose contraries, demolish conventional categories, forcing parallels which are shocking and comparisons which are disconcerting. The manic energy of Gulliver's list in the second half of the first paragraph in chapter 10 drives his alienation from human society at a furious pace, marking out a complete opposition between the utopia of the Houyhnhnms and the dystopia of his native country:

> I enjoyed perfect Health of Body, and Tranquility of Mind; I did not feel the Treachery or Inconstancy of a Friend, nor the Injuries of a secret or open Enemy. I had no Occasion of bribing, flattering or pimping, to procure the Favour of any great Man, or of his Minion. I wanted no Fence against Fraud or Oppression: Here was neither Physician to destroy my Body, nor Lawyer to ruin my Fortune: No Informer to watch my Words and Actions, or forge Accusations against me for Hire: Here were no Gibers, Censurers, Backbiters, Pickpockets, Highwaymen, House-breakers, Attorneys, Bawds, Buffoons, Gamesters, Politicians, Wits, Spleneticks, tedious Talkers, Controvertists, Ravishers, Murderers, Robbers, Virtuoso's; no Leaders or Followers of Party and Faction; no Encouragers to Vice, by Seducement or Examples: No Dungeons, Axes, Gibbets, Whipping-Posts, or Pillories; No cheating Shopkeepers or Mechanicks: No Pride, Vanity or Affectation: No Fops, Bullies, Drunkards, strolling Whores, or Poxes: No ranting, lewd, expensive Wives: No stupid, proud Pedants: No importunate, over-bearing, quarrelsome, noisy, roaring, empty, conceited, swearing Companions: No Scoundrels raised from the Dust upon the Merit of their Vices; or Nobility thrown into it on account of their Virtues: No Lords, Fidlers, Judges or Dancing-masters.   (IV, 10)

Gulliver's utopia is defined by what is missing; he has turned privation into a moral paradise, and the condition under which he thrives is complete separation from his own species. But there is more in this list than a definition of a negative happiness. Gulliver has achieved a state of moral and physical equilibrium by a grotesque caricaturing of his own society. The energy of his denunciation is hysterical and his moral perspective equates trivial irritations ('tedious Talkers', for example) with gross felonies ('Ravishers, Murderers, Robbers'), images of petty swindling with images of torture and endemic disease, incidents of snobbery and examples of social injustice. From Gulliver's point of view, of course, *everything* human is now essentially corrupt, as it was to Swift in strictly orthodox Christian terms. In John Bunyan's *Pilgrim's Progress* (1678) the items of merchandise at Vanity Fair, all of which must be rejected by Christian, include 'Houses, Lands, Trades, Places, Honors, Preferments, Titles, Countries, Kingdoms, Lusts, Pleasures and Delights of all Sorts, as *Whores, Bawds, Wives, Husbands, Children,* Masters, Servants, Lives, Blood, Bodies, Souls, Silver, Gold, Pearls, Precious Stones, and what not' (my italics). As an individual pilgrim, Gulliver's quest is just as rigorous as Christian's, even though his search is characterized in entirely secular terms. The common requirement is rejection of the world, an action taken to secure a better spiritual home. But Swift has substituted the life of Reason for the traditional Christian spiritual purpose. The Houyhnhnm ideal is admirable but insufficient, able to exist only in a fantasy world of talking horses. At its simplest level, Swift's allegory of man's pursuit of Reason neither satirizes that pursuit nor recommends it: if the ideal image of the wholly rational state is a horse-like creature, then that alone suggests the impossibility of attaining the wholly rational state. And if the alternative, in this simplified secular scheme of man's options, is the Yahoo, then man is caught between an ideal which he will fail to attain and a renunciation of that ideal which leads to the anarchy of the jungle. The violent energy of Gulliver's list is a sign of his desperate attempt to deny this paradox of his own nature.

By now it should be clear that when Gulliver praises the Houyhnhnms' concern for 'Friendship and Benevolence . . . Order and Oeconomy' and 'the unerring Rules of Reason' he no longer regards these as human virtues. The Houyhnhnms have a monopoly on certain virtues just as the Yahoos have a monopoly on all vices. Gulliver accordingly is more disgusted by his own reflection in water than by the sight of a Yahoo. He begins to take on horse characteristics, adopting a whine and a trotting gait. This novel attempt by Gulliver to merge with another species proves the cause of his undoing. The Assembly requires his Master either to treat him like a normal Yahoo or get rid of him altogether. Houyhnhnm reason evidently is intolerant of ambiguities like Gulliver. In six weeks Gulliver constructs a canoe from young Yahoo skins and tallow from the same source, apologizes to the reader for the unlikely condescension of the Master in allowing him to kiss his hoof, and sets off.

Initially, Gulliver has no intention of returning to Europe. He prefers a life of permanent isolation on an uninhabited island to life under a 'Yahoo' government. He makes land a short distance due west of the southern tip of Tasmania and is reluctantly rescued by the Portuguese, who conclude that he is deranged.

Gulliver's arbitrary association of man with Yahoo is now examined in dramatic terms, that is, through the agency of a particular character, the first human being whom Gulliver has met for more than four and a half years. Captain Pedro de Mendez is courteous, generous and civil; Gulliver feels 'faint at the very smell of him' (IV, 11). The captain is solicitous, patient, reassuring and wise; Gulliver 'at last . . . descended to treat him like an Animal which had some little Portion of Reason'. The captain delicately introduces Gulliver back to social life, but Gulliver walks in the street with aromatic herbs stuffed up his nostrils. Persuaded to return to England, Gulliver borrows money from the captain and spends the whole of his last voyage closeted in his cabin. Nothing that he has learned among the Houyhnhnms can be transferred to human society. The sight of his family fills him with 'Hatred, Disgust and Contempt . . . And when I began to consider, that by copulating with one of the *Yahoo*-Species, I had become a Parent of more; it struck me with the utmost Shame, Confusion and Horror.' He spurns his family and even after five years of this domestic horror Gulliver will still not permit his food, drink or person to be touched by his Yahoo family. He compensates by spending four hours a day talking to his horses. In all of Gulliver's pompous self-righteousness there is not a grain of humanity, but there is much ironic comedy. His language in this paragraph echoes the words but denies the spirit of the Bible and the *Book of Common Prayer* (the Communion service in particular): 'Saint Paul exhorteth all persons diligently to try and examine themselves, before they presume to eat of that Bread and drink of that Cup . . . We do not presume to come to this thy Table (O merciful Lord) trusting in our own righteousness, but in thy manifold, and great mercyes.' Swift's deft allusion makes Gulliver into God, and a God who is cruelly arrogant.

The final chapter of part IV provides the reader with a statement of Gulliver's purpose in writing and an attack on the gross falsities of the travel-book genre. Once again, Swift provides a subversive commentary on Gulliver's proud claims to veracity. Gulliver quotes a Latin tag from Virgil's *Aeneid* in support of his own truthfulness. But Sinon's words are, in their original context, a preface to his use of the wooden horse against the Trojans. The point, bluntly, is that if you accept what I am saying is true, then look quickly to your own downfall. The more Gulliver protests his own infallibility as a teacher of public morality, the more we suspect his arrogance. Colonialism is his last specific target, and as if to forestall the reader's confidence in condemning Gulliver as insane, his analysis of the motives of imperialism gives pause for thought:

Ships are sent with the first Opportunity; the Natives driven out or destroyed, their Princes tortured to discover their Gold; a free Licence given to all Acts of

> Inhumanity and Lust; the Earth reeking with the Blood of its Inhabitants: And this execrable Crew of Butchers employed in so pious an Expedition, is a *modern Colony* sent to convert and civilize an idolatrous and barbarous People.

This comment on the ideology of imperialism, even though it fits Gulliver's disillusioned image of humanity at this point, also carries the weight of his creator's scorn. A clear signal is the subsequent and extravagantly eulogistic praise of the British nation as the single exception. Swift's years in Ireland since 1714 had been spent in countering the iniquities of English colonialism, and his comment that the British government sends only 'the most vigilant and virtuous Governors [to the colonies] who have no other Views than the Happiness of the People over whom they preside' provides a bleak coda to Gulliver's naivety. But Gulliver has one more trick to play on his gentle readers:

> My Reconcilement to the *Yahoo*-kind in general might not be so difficult, if they would be content with those Vices and Follies only which Nature hath entitled them to. I am not in the least provoked at the Sight of a Lawyer, a Pick-pocket, a Colonel, a Fool, a Lord, a Gamester, a Politician, a Whoremunger, a Physician, an Evidence, a Suborner, an Attorney, a Traytor, or the like: This is all according to the due Course of Things: But, when I behold a Lump of Deformity, and Diseases both in Body and Mind, smitten with *Pride*, it immediately breaks all the Measures of my Patience; neither shall I ever be able to comprehend how such an Animal and such a Vice could tally together . . . I dwell the longer upon this Subject from the Desire I have to make the Society of an *English Yahoo* by any means not insupportable; and therefore I here intreat those who have any Tincture of this absurd Vice, that they will not presume to appear in my Sight.

Gulliver's toleration of a corrupt humanity has grown, but it is still a confused amalgam of Olympian holier-than-thou arrogance and comi-tragic despair. The only word to describe this parting gesture to the reader is also the name of the vice which Gulliver so bitterly declaims against: Pride. Swift's implicit charge against Gulliver is that only a man who has failed to know *himself* can exempt himself from a universal failing. Gulliver leaves us, therefore, with a ringing denunciation of himself as well as a stinging rebuke. If our Reason is only used to exacerbate our natural corruption, there is yet a greater error in believing that we can rise above the common paradox of man's nature. When we read Pope's *Essay on Man* those paradoxes have the pristine clarity of doctrine; reading *Gulliver's Travels* we experience the constant, sometimes electrifying psychological anguish of a character who perceives the insoluble paradoxes and persuades himself that they can be transcended. If we recall Swift's poem *The Place of the Damn'd*, printed five years after the publication of *Gulliver's Travels*, the lineaments of Gulliver's

journey to a self-enclosed arrogance are once more revealed with a
colloquial familiarity which freezes our self-possession:

All Folks who pretend to Religion *and* Grace,
Allow there's a HELL, *but dispute of the Place;*
But if HELL *by Logical Rules be defin'd,*
The Place of the Damn'd, – *I'll tell you my Mind.*
  Wherever the Damn'd do Chiefly abound,
Most certainly there's the HELL *to be found,*
Damn'd Poets, *Damn'd* Criticks, *Damn'd* Block-Heads, *Damn'd* Knaves,
Damn'd Senators *brib'd, Damn'd prostitute* Slaves;
Damn'd Lawyers *and* Judges, *Damn'd* Lords *and Damn'd* Squires,
Damn'd Spies *and* Informers, *Damn'd* Friends *and Damn'd* Lyars;
Damn'd Villains, *Corrupted in every* Station,
Damn'd Time-Serving Priests *all over the* Nation;
And into the Bargain, I'll readily give you
Damn'd Ignorant Prelates, *and Councellors Privy.*
Then let us no longer by Parsons *be Flam'd,*
For We know by these Marks, *the Place of the Damn'd;*
And HELL to be sure is at Paris *or* Rome,
How happy for Us, *that it is not at* Home.

(Poems, I I, 575–6)

As Swift imagines the world in *The Day of Judgement* (1731), the same
solipsism is shattered, this time by Jehovah himself:

  '*Offending Race of Human Kind,*
  By Nature, Reason, Learning, blind;
  You who thro' Frailty step'd aside,
  And you who never fell – thro' *Pride;*
  You who in different Sects have shamm'd,
  And come to see each other damn'd;
  (*So some Folks told you, but they knew*
  No more of Jove's Designs than you)
  And I resent these Pranks no more.
  I to such Blockheads set my Wit!
  I damn such fools! – Go, go, you're bit.'*

(Poems, I I, 578–9)

Gulliver's *final* act is to add a letter to his publisher, Cousin Sympson,
written 'seven Months' after publication of the *Travels* and first printed

---

* i.e. deceived.

in Faulkner's 1735 edition. In spite of his despair at the incorrigibility of the Yahoo species in I V, 12, Gulliver here expresses his dismay that his book has failed to eradicate vice at least from England in these few weeks. Swift's *initial* act, then, as the source of this letter, is to expose the arrogance of authorship once more, as he had done in *A Tale of a Tub*. To this extent Gulliver is enclosed within Swift's general onslaught on the mendacity of travel-writers and the credulity of readers. Although the genre of the travel-book is the most obvious structural feature of the *Travels*, there are other scaffolds on which Swift hangs Gulliver.

4 Sources and their Transformation

They say that if Circe had offered Ulysses two potions, the one to make a madman wise, and the other to make a wise man mad, Ulysses would rather have taken a cup of madness than consent to Circe's transforming his human shape into that of a beast; and they add that Wisdom herself would have spoken to him in this wise: 'Forgive me, let me alone, rather than allow me to dwell in the body and shape of an ass.'
Montaigne, *Apology for Raimond Sebond* (1603)

Swift's use of existing literary materials for *Gulliver's Travels* shows an eclectic mind working over a well-established idea with a fresh and invigorated novelty of imagination. Apart from well-known parodies of travellers' tales, such as Lucian's *True History* already mentioned, the general outline of the genre's potential for questioning moral insularity is well illustrated by the following example from the work of one of Swift's occasional targets, Richard Boyle, the father of modern chemistry. Boyle's *Occasional Reflections upon Several Subjects* (1664) was itself prompted by the conventionality of the travel-book and alludes to two key works of utopian speculative writing. As in *Gulliver's Travels*, the interest here is in the relativity of national views:

EUGENIUS: 'You put me in mind of a fancy of your friend Mr *Boyle*, who was saying, that he had thoughts of making a short romantick story, where the scene should be laid in some island of the southern ocean, governed by some such rational laws and customs, as those of *Utopia* or the *New Atlantis*; and, in this country, he would introduce an observing native, that, upon his return home from his travels in *Europe*, should give an account of our countries and manners under feigned names, and frequently intimate in his relations, (or in his answers to questions that should be made to him) the reasons of his wondering to find our customs so extravagant, and differing from those of our country. For your friend imagined, that by such a way of proposing many of our practices, we should ourselves be brought unawares to condemn, or perhaps laugh at them, and should at least cease to wonder, to find other nations think them as extravagant, as we think the manners of the Dutch and Spaniards, as they are represented in our travellers books.

LINDAMOR: I dislike not the project, and wish it were prosecuted by somebody, that, being impartial, were more a friend to fables. For when I consider, that the name of Barbarian was given by the two noblest people of the earth, the Greeks and the Romans, not only to all the rest of the world, but to one another, though both these nations were highly civilized, and the courtly Persians, and other voluptuous Asiaticks, were perhaps no less than they; I doubt, that most nations, in styling one another's manners extravagant and absurd, are guided more by education and partiality, than reason; and that we laugh at many customs of strangers, only because we never considered them. And we may well believe, that custom has a much larger empire, than men seem to be well aware of, since whole nations are wholly swayed by it, that do not reckon themselves among its subjects, nor so much as dream, that they are so.

Whether or not Swift's reading of Boyle's *Reflections* included this passage, it was a prescient anticipation of the *Travels*, particularly Lindamor's point that those most prejudiced are least able to discern their own myopia. Literary travel overseas seems necessarily to include comparison with one's own cultural presuppositions. A century later, in 1768, Sterne's *A Sentimental Journey* offered a taxonomy of traveller-types (eleven in all, including the Splenetic Traveller, such as Smollett, whose book was 'nothing but the account of his miserable feelings'), as 'an assay upon human nature'. Its doctrine of social optimism and universal benevolence is an exact antithesis to Gulliver's final misanthropy. Whereas Gulliver exchanges the rational culture of the Houyhnhnms for the home-grown product, Sterne writes: '*Le* POUR *et le* CONTRE *se trouvent en chaque nation*; there is a balance . . . of good and bad every where; and nothing but the knowing it is so can emancipate one half of the world from the prepossessions which it holds against the other . . . the advantage of travel, as it regarded the *sçavoir vivre*, was by seeing a great deal of both men and manners; it taught us mutual toleration; and mutual toleration . . . taught us mutual love.'

In 1551 Sir Thomas More's *Utopia* was translated into English. Its traveller-hero is Raphael Hythloday, a Renaissance combination of Ulysses and Plato, a scholar of Greek literature and a philosopher. In other respects he is more like Gulliver. He undertakes four voyages, the first three with Amerigo Vespucci, but after the final voyage out to the well-ordered land of Utopia (a name which means both 'no place' and also 'beautiful place'), where he lives for five years, he decides not to return to his home in Antwerp. Like Gulliver, he is eventually brought back in a Portuguese ship, and thereafter lives out his days bridling at the indocibility of mankind. Also like Gulliver he ends his dialogue with the reader (More himself is the internal and politely sceptical interlocutor) with a sermon on Pride, 'the root of all evil . . . this servant of hell slithers into the hearts of mankind and there like the bloodsucker prevents men from improving their lot' (II, 95). There are substantial differences between the respective methods and styles of More and Swift, and Swift could gain nothing from a *direct* parody of More's work. The former is controlled, urbane, methodical, gently ironic, doubtless influenced by Plato's *Republic* for some ideas and for its style of dialogue. Gulliver's climactic essay on Pride is craggy, violent, unpredictable, shocking, and crashes through all social and rhetorical decorums. Apart from the innumerable echoes of structure and theme it is this verbal frenzy which gives Swift's book its unique and dazzling energy. Unlike *Utopia*, there is no attempt to frame the discussion by an authorial civility of address. Moreover, for all its communistic theory about the abolition of private property (not to mention money and lawyers), the Utopians and the book in which they are described have an overt religious purpose and guiding principle, as *Gulliver's Travels* does not. The Utopians worship a god incomprehensible to human reason (Mithra) and define virtue as 'living according to the dictates of nature' (II, 70); but unlike the similarly motivated Houyhnhnms they also believe that the power of reason is in itself insufficient for the virtuous life: 'The ultimate truth attained by human reason must be aided by revelation to find a better' (II, 74). Only in the *past* did the Lilliputians hold that 'the Disbelief of a Divine Providence renders a Man uncapable of holding any publick Station' (I, 6). Hythloday argues a seductive case for a *better* social organization; Gulliver's loathing of humanity accepts nothing but a wholesale substitution. War, greed, disease, factional religions, and the iniquity of standing armies in peacetime are all major themes in both books, but the difference in treatment lies in the degree of moral realism needed to counteract them. More himself corrects the moral indignation of Hythloday with these cautionary words:

You do not, simply because you are unable to uproot mistaken opinions and correct long-established ills, abandon the state altogether. In a storm you do not desert the ship because you are unable to control the winds. Nor should you, on the other hand, impose unwelcome advice upon people whom you know to be of opposite mind. You must try to use subtle and indirect means, insofar as it lies in your power. And what you cannot turn to good, you must make as little evil as possible. To have everything turn out well assumes that all men are good, and this is a situation that I do not expect to come about for many years. (II, 48–9)

Gulliver, we should recall, was convinced that 'seven Months were a sufficient Time to correct every Vice and Folly to which *Yahoos* are subject' (letter to Sympson), and by comparison with More's sceptical optimism Gulliver's rage seems childishly naive.

For his principled stand against oppression Swift regarded More as 'the only man of true virtue that ever England produced' (*Prose Works*,

V, 247), and in III, 7 More is the *only* post-classical figure in Brutus's sextumvirate of heroes. Like Sir William Temple, the man and his work offered role models, perhaps, but in working over the territory covered by *Utopia* Swift was also driven by the satirist's need to strike beyond the limits of a philosophical argument, to whip up his readers' indignation by showing them a traveller foolish enough to believe that human ingenuity might, just once, divert its energy from self-aggrandisement and take the path of moral reformation.

No single text or idea is sufficient in itself to control Swift's purposes in *Gulliver's Travels.* Swift borrowed from anywhere if it suited the particular moment. At its simplest level, the whole of the second paragraph of II, 1 (a concentrated burst of nautical jargon) was lifted almost verbatim from Samuel Sturmy's *Mariner's Magazine* (1669), an example of the textbook authenticity of the travel-book; but when the theft is recognized, it becomes an oblique hit against Gulliver's oft-argued veracity. At the other extreme, Swift used certain literary techniques which have no specific literary proprietorship at all, and the broadest of these is allegory.

Swift's use of allegorical means to satirize his own society is neither simple nor consistent. Most critics readily associate Flimnap with Sir Robert Walpole, Queen Anne's Chief (or Prime) Minister, though officially he was Chancellor of the Exchequer. Reldresal, Gulliver's friend at the Lilliputian court, has been variously identified as the Earl of Stanhope (leader of the Whig government from 1717 to 1721), as Lord Carteret, Principal Secretary of State from 1721 to 1724, and as Lord Townshend, Whig Secretary of State and a friend of Swift. Skyris Bolgolam (Admiral of the Realm and Gulliver's leading prosecutor) has been interpreted as an image of Queen Anne's great general, the Duke of Marlborough, or as the Earl of Nottingham, First Lord of the Admiralty (1680–84) but of no competence in naval matters and vindictive towards his successor, Harley. Of places rather than people, the Lilliputian capital (Mildendo) may be a version of London; the neighbouring country of Blefuscu may be France. In the second voyage it has been suggested that Gulliver's gigantic nurse is based (tenuously, one hopes) on the character of Stella; that Lorlbrulgrad may be a version of London. The King of Brobdingnag strikes some commentators as an image of William III, others as the Prince of Wales, or a reflection of Sir William Temple. In the third voyage Lindalino quite clearly is an image of Dublin's resistance to England's attempt to impose Wood's coinage on Ireland. For Lord Munodi the candidates have included Bolingbroke, Lord Middleton (who had opposed the imposition of the coinage), Harley (when Earl of

Oxford), and Temple. The Academy of Lagado quite clearly reflects a distorted image of the Royal Society (as well as borrowing from the Kingdom of the Quintessence in Rabelais's *Gargantua and Pantagruel* and from other literary models such as the House of Solomon in Bacon's *New Atlantis*). In III, 7, Maldonada is again London; Glubbdubdrib may be Dublin; Luggnagg may be England. There are no *individual* candidates offered for the roles of Yahoo and Houyhnhnm, of course, but some commentators have suggested Swift's response to the Irish is reflected in the first and that the Houyhnhnms may be a satirical image of the rational theology of the Deists. What is clear is that the first two voyages are very largely where the question of individual and politically topical reference arises, whereas the third and fourth voyages are increasingly taken up with satire of general ideas.

It would be foolish to read *Gulliver's Travels* as a *roman à clef*, or even as a specific allegorical account of Swift's own life. Swift's imagination surely proceeded from specific and local irritants but expressed itself in general terms when he wished to reach a wide audience. Even though the first voyage alludes in some detail to the events of English political history between 1708 and 1715 (and, centrally, to the Treaty of Utrecht), its continued survival and permanent comedy as literary satire can hardly be said to depend on historical footnoting. Swift warned Pope that because of its dense topical allusiveness *The Dunciad* would be unintelligible twenty miles outside London. He insisted that the names of the dunces should be restored to the text. In spite of what is said in *Verses on the Death of Dr Swift*, i.e. that Swift 'lash'd the Vice but spar'd the Name', when Swift wanted to name names he did so, as the *Verses* themselves make abundantly clear. In *The Drapier's Letters* he not only repeatedly named William Wood as the instrument of an iniquitous English policy, he pillories and puns upon his name with gusto. The effect is not only to expose Wood himself but to inflate and ridicule him as a puppet and a tool of a political system. Equally, no contemporary reader would think of identifying the term 'Great Man' or 'Prime Minister' with anybody but Walpole. Under various soubriquets, Walpole figures as Flimnap in Swift, Macheath in Gay's *The Beggar's Opera* (1728), Pisistratus and Pericles in Bolingbroke's *On the Policy of the Athenians* (1732), and as the eponymous hero of Henry Fielding's novel, *Jonathan Wild* (1743). If the target was obvious, too much specificity would spoil the point, as well as running the risk of legal action against author and publisher. Such was the popularity of parallel histories, political allegories and fables, in fact, that their allusiveness could become a matter of complaint at their transparency rather than their mystification. A month after the appearance of *Gulliver's Travels*, Nicholas Amhurst ('Caleb D'anvers') wrote in the anti-Walpole journal *The Craftsman*, No. 7:

The Application of Passages of the *Roman* Story to our Times is become so common and trite a Way of satirizing the Persons of the present Age, that no Man, who has a tolerable Genius, or the least Invention of his own, will condescend to it. How easy it is to turn over *Tully*, *Tacitus*, or *Livy* and when you have found a good strong Sentence or two upon *Corruption*, to insert it in any Paper? The Author need never be at the trouble to make an Application. Every Child in the Street knows well enough upon whom to fix it.

Running against the tide of Gulliver's veracity and his circumstantial account of 'actual' exotic countries, institutions and personalities is the stronger current of Swift's determination to pillory the accepted conventions of European life. The allegory which bridges these two currents is both particular and generic, and sometimes simultaneously so. When Flimnap–Walpole capers on the tightrope at least an inch higher than anybody else, or performs somersaults at court, we do not need to be told that Swift's political satire fits a Whig Prime Minister better than a Tory. The mode of the satire is clearly generic: *all* politicians of whatever political persuasion are prone to perform in public for the sake of their own advancement, and it is the wise philosopher, the King of Brobdingnag, who laughs with cosmic irony at the supremely irrelevant question of whether Gulliver is a Whig or a Tory. Swift's image of them both suggests that to define a man's whole being by one of two public labels is as absurd as defining a man's religion by the height of his shoe-heels. The *psychology* of faction is the target here, not the particular political label. In the *Sentiments of a Church of England Man* (1708) Swift saw trouble from both parties: 'I should think that, in order to preserve the Constitution entire in Church and State, whoever hath a true Value for both, would be sure to avoid the Extremes of Whig for the sake of the former, and the Extremes of Tory on account of the latter.' In practice, however, the *realpolitik* of Swift's own time was oppressively and decisively characterized along two-party lines. In her speech from the throne in May 1702 Queen Anne prayed to be free of Whig and Tory power-struggles. In his *History of my Own Time* the Whig Bishop Burnet claimed that in 1708 'in every corner of the nation the two parties stand, as it were listed against one another'. The incendiary preacher Henry Sacheverell was charged at his trial in 1710 with keeping up 'a distinction of faction and parties'. Several years after the Tories fell from office, Pope wrote in 1717 that 'the Parties of Walpole and Stanhope are as violent as Whig and Tory'. The party issue could itself be a political weapon, and in 1722–3 occurred an event which provided Swift with perhaps the most topically detailed incident in *Gulliver's Travels*, the treason trial of his long-standing friend Francis Atterbury, Bishop of Rochester and Dean of Westminster. Atterbury was accused of conspiring to restore the Catholic Pretender ('James III') to the English throne, and during his widely discussed and reported trial evidence from paid informers and cryptographers was used against him. In chapter 6 of the third voyage Gulliver volunteers a thinly veiled account of the system of political espionage in Langden (London) in the kingdom of Tribnia (Britain) – two of the simplest and, in the latter case, most transparent anagrams. in the whole of the *Travels*. As an example of the political cryptographers' work, '*Our Brother* Tom *has just got the Piles*' decodes as '*Resist, – a Plot is brought home – The Tour*'. By such ingenious means the lowest informer can topple or prop a whole administration with total impunity and in absolute secrecy:

It is first agreed and settled among them, what suspected Persons shall be accused of a Plot: Then, effectual Care is taken to secure all their Letters and other Papers, and put the Owners in Chains. These Papers are delivered to a Set of Artists very dextrous in finding out the mysterious Meanings of Words, Syllables and Letters. For Instance, they can decypher a Close-stool to signify a Privy-Council; a Flock of Geese, a Senate; a lame Dog, an Invader; the Plague, a standing Army; a Buzard, a Minister; the Gout, a High Priest; a Gibbet, a Secretary of State; a Chamber pot, a Committee of Grandees; a Sieve, a Court Lady; a Broom, a Revolution; a Mouse-trap, an Employment; a bottomless Pit, the Treasury; a Sink, a C—t; a Cap and Bells, a Favourite; a broken Reed, a Court of Justice; an empty Tun, a General; a running Sore, the Administration.

(III, 6)

Although some of these very terms had been produced in evidence at Atterbury's trial, two aspects of Swift's satirical transformation should be noted. At no point is the guilt or innocence of the historical Atterbury Swift's concern; and secondly, the list of examples is itself an autonomous parody of perfectly obvious mischievous transferences. The list Gulliver gives us lacks the baffling arbitrariness of a real code-system because Swift's eye is on communicating the transparently criminal stupidity of those who run a government using such means. Fascinating as it is to see Swift working with actual historical materials, and important as this is to an understanding of Swift's satirical imagination, historical authenticity itself neither explains nor produces the enduring comedy of Swift's political allegory.

Swift's least stimulating satire stays closest to its sources. The ridicule of scientific experiments in III, 5 has an antiquarian comic interest but is also so patently absurd that it leaves neither Gulliver nor the reader a role to play except that of a circus spectator around the ring of cavorting clowns. Swift changes very little in order to convert the actual into the fantastic, and this conversion required nothing but a superficial knowledge on Swift's part. Moreover, it was part of Sprat's own apologia in his *History of the Royal Society* to dissociate 'serious' science from the lunatic fringe who continued to square the circle, search for the philosopher's stone, and seek to turn base metals into gold. Even so, Gulliver's first encounter in the Academy of Lagado is with a Man who 'had been Eight Years upon a Project for extracting Sun-beams out of Cucumbers, which were to be put into Vials hermetically sealed, and let out to warm the Air in raw inclement Summers' (III, 5). During the 1720s Pope's clerical neighbour Stephen Hales had been conducting research on the effects of sunshine on plant respiration. His reports were read to the Royal Society, and in 1726/7 he published a volume entitled *Vegetable Staticks*. The twentieth experiment in chapter 1 includes this passage:

The scorching heat of a hot bed of horse-dung, when too hot for plants, is 75 degrees and more, and hereabout is probably the heat of the blood in high fevers.

The due healthy heat of a hot bed of horse-dung, in the fine mold, where the roots of thriving Cucumber-plants were, in *Feb.* was 56 degrees, which is nearly the bosom-heat, and that for the hatching of eggs. The heat of the air under the glass-frame of this hot-bed was 34 degrees; so the roots had 26 degrees more heat, than the plants above ground. The heat of the open air was then 17 degrees . . . The impulse of the Sun-beams giving the moisture of the earth a brisk undulating motion, which watery particles, when separated and rarified by heat, do ascend in the form of vapour: And the vigour of warm and confined vapour, (such as is that which is 1, 2, or 3 feet deep in the earth) must be very considerable, so as to penetrate the roots with some vigour . . . If plants were not in this manner supported with moisture, it were impossible for them to subsist, under the scorching heats, within the tropicks, where they have no rain for many months together.

The difficulty about ridiculing science on the basis of an undisclosed but nevertheless reactionary moral principle is that although modern scientists are only rarely concerned with ethics, scientists in the early eighteenth century certainly were. Observation and measurement of physical phenomena could confirm one's faith in a metaphysical origin and principle in the world's processes. Perhaps Swift intuitively anticipated a future divergence of science and morality, but the pious rector of Teddington saw no conflict whatsoever. In his introduction to *Vegetable Staticks*, he claimed:

The farther researches we make into this admirable scene of things, the more beauty and harmony we see in them: And the stronger and clearer convictions they give us, of the being, power and wisdom of the divine Architect, who has made all things to concur with a wonderful conformity, in carrying on, by various and innumerable combinations of matter, such a circulation of causes, and effects, as was necessary to the great ends of nature.

And since we are assured that the all-wise Creator has observed the most exact proportions, of *number, weight and measure*, in the make of all things; the most likely way therefore, to get any insight into the nature of those parts of the creation, which come within our observation, must in all reason be to number, weight and measure.

Invoking history, either in an argument about originality or madness, may prove a double-edged weapon. Having calculated the temperature of cucumber roots, Hales makes an aside about the 'modern [*sic*] invention to convey heated air into rooms thro' hot flues'. Hales had forgotten about the Roman hypocaust, just as Swift's ridicule of the Laputian astronomers was to backfire in 1877, when the second satellite around Mars was indeed proved a reality. To Swift, if not to the modern microbiologist, it is intrinsically absurd for a man to fix his thoughts and talents on the study of a flea seen through a microscope. He should be better employed on moral philosophy. We would not wish to argue that the two are mutually exclusive, but Swift's view is astonishingly categorical. All his experimenters are suffering from an *absence* of mind, if we define the mind's proper function as the discrimination of moral questions. Swift defines all science by its lunatic fringe, it seems, and is unwilling to concede that the essence of experimental activity lies precisely in trial, error, hypothesis, guesswork, inquisitiveness, and speculation beyond the constraints of social need. Already out of step and sympathy with the new science, Swift's satire of it looked even further back, to the technique of Dryden's Zimri portrait in *Absalom and Achitophel*, where the amateur mind skims along the surface of several discrete activities, driven by whimsy and restlessness:

> *in the course of one revolving Moon,*
> *Was Chymist, Fidler, States-Man, and Buffoon:*
> *Then all for Women, Painting, Rhiming, Drinking;*
> *Besides ten thousand Freaks that dy'd in thinking.*
> *Blest Madman, who coud every hour employ,*
> *With something New to wish, or to enjoy!* (ll. 549–54)

Naming a specific satiric target both particularizes and limits the satiric effect. Allegory escapes this fate only to run the opposite risk of allowing

73

the possibility of a multiplicity of identifications to be made. But if allegory submerges the particular in the general, a positive gain may be that previously unintended candidates may emerge to fit the satirist's bill. If the allegory is good enough it will attract broad applications and outlive its topicality. In III, 3, Gulliver encounters the Flying Island, describes its measurements, function, construction, means of propulsion, and includes a diagram of its track across the island of Balnibarbi. The Flying Island is the most specific and detailed of all the scientific phenomena described in the third voyage, and its critical interpretation as allegory shows its simultaneously specific and general significance. Abel Boyer summarized *Gulliver's Travels* immediately on its publication in *The Political State of Great Britain* (November to January 1726–7). He rightly observed that the Academy of Lagado was 'intended to expose and ridicule the *follies* and *whimsies* of . . . *crack brained experimental philosophers*', and pointed out in general terms Swift's indebtedness to Plato's *Republic*, More's *Utopia*, Bacon's *New Atlantis*, Rabelais's *Gargantua and Pantagruel*, and D'Alais's *History of the Severambi* (1677–9). He also remarked that 'As to his *allusions*, and allegories they are, for the most part so strong, so glaring and so obvious, that a man must be a great stranger to the world, in general, and to *courtiers, statesmen, corrupt senators, rakes of quality, lawyers, physicians, virtuosi, soldiers, sharpers,* and *women* [*sic*!] in particular to have need of a *key*' (quoted in Ehrenpreis III, 503). Others did not think Swift's allegory was so obvious, it should be said, including members of Swift's own circle. Boyer, however, suggested that the Flying Island stands for the royal prerogative, an image of the abuse of power to intimidate a subject people. Historians of science noticed in 1937 that the Flying Island seemed to be based on the *terella* or little earth described in William Gilbert's *De Magnete* (1600), a spherical loadstone designed to show the magnetic field of the earth, an example of which was exhibited in the Royal Society (Nicolson and Mohler, p. 252). None of Swift's contemporaries pointed out the specific allusion, if they noticed it at all. To us in the twentieth century, as to Boyer in the eighteenth, Swift's image is more cogent as an example of the misuse of (technological) means in the pursuit of political domination, a prefiguring of Star Wars technology. The point is, of course, that Swift's imagination has transcended both sources and detailed allusion to create meanings larger than the sum of the individual parts. Some of Swift's contemporary readers not only expected the satire to work in this general way, but were gratified to see it do so. Pope declared: 'I find no considerable man very angry at the book: some indeed think it rather too bold, and too general a satire: but

none that I hear of accuse it of particular reflections (I mean no persons
of consequence, or good judgment; the mob of critics, you know, always
are desirous to apply satire to those that they envy for being above
them) so that you needed not to have been so secret upon this head.'
And John Gay reported (doubtless with a fully intentional fine irony)
that: 'The politicians to a man agree, that it is free from particular
reflections, but that the satire on general societies of men is too severe'
(*Correspondence of Alexander Pope*, II, 412). Gay also expected keys
from the reductive and mischievous minds of the critics, but it seems to
have been Bolingbroke who first raised the deeper question of Swift's
motives in such a general satire. According to Gay's report, Bolingbroke
was 'the person who least approves it, blaming it as a design of evil
consequence to depreciate human nature'. Finding sources for Swift's
fable is a continuing industry, though not all its practitioners will admit
that once a source has been established we are any the wiser as to Swift's
'intended' meanings. Both Swift's reading and experience provided no
more than the raw materials for a conversion and a metamorphosis
which took place in his unique imagination. Something of this was in
Bolingbroke's mind when he wrote that 'Pope and you are very great
Wits, and I think very indifferent Philosophers' (*Correspondence*, 10
December 1725). Bolingbroke championed reason as the only necessary
guide to the life of the mind. Swift showed its precariousness not through
philosophic means but through a comic fable. The link between the
classic Deist position on rational virtue and Swift's depiction of its error
and insufficiency in the fourth voyage is not in the similarity of ideas
being promoted but in Swift's remorseless conviction that the admirable
theory is hopelessly out of touch with the oppressive reality. Man should
be rational, but his actions prove otherwise, and in the figures of the
Yahoo and the Houyhnhnm Swift produced a psychic horror of peculiar
intensity for the Age of Reason. In William Wollaston's *The Religion of
Nature Delineated* (1725) the Deist theologian worked over the age-old
paradox of man's nature in *terms*, though not in imaginative power,
quite close to Swift:

... how wretchedly do they violate the *order* of nature, and transgress against
truth, who not only *reject* the conduct of reason to follow sense and passion, but
even make it subservient to them; who use it only in finding out means to effect
their wicked ends, or the nature of those means, whether they are just or unjust,
right or *wrong*? This is not only to *deviate* from the path of nature, but to *invert* it,
and to become something *more* than *brutish*; *brutes with reason*, which must be
the most enormous and worst of all brutes. When the *brute* is governed by sense
and bodily appetites, he observes *his proper* rule; when a *man* is governed after

that manner in defiance of his reason, he *violates* his: but when he makes his rational powers to *serve* the brutish part, to assist and promote it, he heightens and increases the *brutality*, inlarges its field, makes it to act with greater force and effect, and becomes a *monster* . . .

Wollaston chastises those who fall beneath the expected norms of reason and holds out to them a finer Christian alternative. In *Gulliver's Travels* the monster has become the human norm and government by secular rationality an unattainable ideal. This is not philosophy, and neither is it Christian; but its satirical power is devastating. Gulliver, the rational theologians and the Houyhnhnms are all in error: if man's rationality is permanently flawed, it is absurd to worship only that which is intelligible. Gulliver makes man a marginal creature, but Swift makes Gulliver the fool of his reason.

5 Styles, Language and Rhetoric

Proper Words in proper Places, makes the true Definition of a Style. But this would require too ample a Disquisition to be now dwelt on ... When a Man's Thoughts are clear, the properest Words will generally offer themselves first, and his own Judgment will direct him in what Order to place them, so as they may be best understood. Where Men err against this Method, it is usually on purpose, and to show their Learning, their Oratory, their Politeness, or their Knowledge of the World. In short, that Simplicity, without which no human Performance can arrive to any great Perfection, is no where more eminently useful than this.

This definition of style comes from Swift's *Letter to a Young Gentleman, Lately Enter'd into Holy Orders* (1720), and is itself subject to its own theory of rhetoric. One would hardly advise an intended priest to be anything other than clear, intelligible, honest, and not to baffle his congregation with far-sought learning. As for a *general* definition of Swift's style, it is misleadingly simple. Swift is the master of *styles*, a brilliant impersonator of the many registers and dialects of the written word, each of which is determined by the occasion, the purpose, the intended audience, and the speaker. In his satires any piece of literary language from Swift is likely to be coloured by the dramatic viewpoint. In another sense, however, what Swift says above is entirely accurate. A speaker's mind *is* revealed by the language he uses. The question is only whether he reveals more or less than he intends, either through ignorance or dishonesty. Swift praised Sir William Temple for skilfully matching his style to the correspondent in the 'art' of the informal letter. In *The Drapier's Letters* Swift faced a multiplicity of audiences and wrote according to his perception of their different interests, loyalties, and intellectual abilities. *Letters* I and IV were addressed to the whole people of Ireland, 'Tradesmen, Shop-Keepers, Farmers, and Country-People in General', and Swift's rhetoric is blunt, explanatory, and reassuringly framed by scriptural parallels and patriotic exhortation: 'I do most earnestly exhort you as *Men*, as *Christians*, as *Parents*, and as *Lovers of your Country*, to read this Paper with the utmost Attention, or get it read to you by others; which that you may do at the less Expence, I have ordered the Printer to sell it at the lowest Rate ... Therefore, my Friends, stand to it One and All: Refuse this *Filthy Trash*. It is no Treason to rebel against Mr *Wood*. His *Majesty* in his Patent obliges no body to take these Half-pence' (*Prose Works*, X, 3, 11). A later address, *Some*

Observations . . . relating to Wood's Half-pence, is by contrast addressed to the educated nobility and gentry of Ireland. Keeping up the by now transparent disguise of an under-educated shopkeeper, who argues without 'Art, Cunning, or Eloquence', the Drapier nevertheless discusses legal and other theoretical arguments, analyses documents, and cites legal authorities, all designed to worry the vested interest of landowners and stimulate their 'English' constitutional consciences. *A Tale of a Tub*, as we have seen, sub-divides its audience into three categories, aiming itself at the *Learned*, and through its own obscurity mirrors the imputed taste of its targets. In *Gulliver's Travels* there is the widest range of styles, matching Gulliver's various functions as both autonomous character and manipulated satirical mouthpiece. When he needs to speak like a mariner, Swift gives him a slab of nautical jargon lifted straight from the *Mariner's Magazine*; when he is in the company of the Lagadian Projectors, he speaks like one of them (as in his description of the Flying Island); he takes on the style of the Olympian King of Brobdingnag when he addresses us in part IV; he apes the views and even the trotting gait of his Houyhnhnm masters.

Like his creator, Gulliver is a chameleon of styles. It might be thought that Swift's use of the persona, or mask, is the key to Swift's strategies and meanings, and that a simple process of reversing what the satirical mask says will produce the true Swiftian viewpoint: for negative read positive. But one of the most vexing characteristics of Swift's satire is that it seems no part of his strategy to leave clear space between the speaker (or persona) and the 'author'. Swift moves in and out of his dramatic constructions without warning, and the effect is destabilizing on both created character and reader alike. The marks of Swift's *presence* are sometimes signalled by no more than a phrase, a tone of voice, or something as 'neutral' as a type-face. Five paragraphs from the end of *A Modest Proposal* there are ten practical and orthodox economic proposals for remedying the sickness of Ireland. All of them are dismissed as useless and visionary in the present plight of Ireland, and all of them had been seriously proposed by Swift and others in numerous tracts written during the 1720s (for a list, see *An Humble Address to Parliament, Prose Works*, X, 128–9):

I desire the Reader will observe, that I calculate my Remedy *for this one individual Kingdom of I R E L A N D, and for no Other that ever was, is, or I think, ever can be upon Earth.* Therefore let no man talk to me of other Expedients: *Of taxing our Absentees at five Shillings a Pound: Of using neither Cloaths, nor Household Furniture, except what is of our own Growth and Manufacture: Of utterly rejecting the Materials and Instruments that promote Foreign Luxury: Of curing the*

Expensiveness of Pride, Vanity, Idleness, and Gaming in our Women: Of intro-ducing a Vein of Parcimony, Prudence and Temperance: Of learning to love our Country . . .

The ostensible purpose of the rhetoric here is to define the ailments of Ireland as utterly resistant to 'normal' economic medicine. It also pro-ceeds to divulge the root cause as neither economic nor political, but moral. In dismissing his own economic proposals Swift points to a unique misery which is beyond the reach of orthodox principles, but firmly in the province of the preacher. A sign of this shift is the liturgical cadence in the second half of the first sentence, a syntactic signal of the preacher leaning over the shoulder of the ironist. Swift wrote to Pope without rhetorical inversions on 11 August 1729:

As to this country, there have been three terrible years dearth of corn, and every place strowed with beggars, but dearths are common in better climates, and our evils here lie much deeper. Imagine a nation the two-thirds of whose revenues are spent out of it, and who are not permitted to trade with the other third, and where the pride of the women will not suffer them to wear their own manufactures even where they excel what come from abroad: This is the true state of Ireland in a very few words. These evils operate more every day, and the Kingdom is absolutely undone, as I have been telling it often in print these ten years past.

(*Correspondence*, III, 341)

Again, Swift's mind runs on economic facts before concluding with a moral roll-call, and what might *seem* to be a gratuitous and characteristic hit at the pride of women in the *Proposal* here turns out to be a serious economic point. In the first passage our eyes are captured by the typo-graphical prominence of *useless* proposals, and we interpret this as a bitter irony. In the letter to Pope there is no need for 'interpretation', even though similar points are being established. The satirical version in the *Proposal* clearly works harder by involving the reader as judge. If reasonable and otherwise universally valid economic laws are hopeless, then Swift both offers and rejects them at the same time. We are given the choice between denying Ireland common treatment with other civil-ized nations, or conniving in a monstrous 'final solution'. On another occasion a different kind of rhetoric shows what Swift might *actually* believe, this time in relation to England's economic problems:

The true way of multiplying Mankind to public Advantage in such a Country as *England*, is . . . To enact and enforce Sumptuary Laws against Luxury, and all Excesses in Cloathing, Furniture, and the like: To encourage Matrimony, and reward, as the *Romans* did, those who have a certain Number of Children.

(*The History of the Four Last Years of the Queen, Prose Works*, VI, 95)

But if the Modest Proposer is inhuman, this seems totalitarian. It has all of the simplistic clarity of the Houyhnhnms and all of the moral arbitrariness of a Puritan. We might ask how Swift can assert the needs of the state over the rights of the individual in such a way and at the same time put himself forward as the defender of Irish liberties.

Mocking his own seriousness, Swift signals the wit constrained by the preacher, the joker disciplined by the moralist, and of the Establishment man at odds with the radical outsider. Such tensions distinguish the nervous and unstable rhetoric of Swift's satire from the elegant, sharply-focused and integrated paradoxes of the confident and didactic satire of Pope in, for example, the *Essay on Man*. Whereas Pope describes and shapes the paradoxes of man's nature into a definitive and artistically stable whole, Swift leaves the paradoxes unresolved, jagged, awkward, and often violently in conflict. Gulliver's 'positives', i.e. patriotism, veracity, reforming moral zeal, and his high moral tone, are neither intrinsically ridiculous nor are they things which Swift elsewhere disassociated from his own public position. However much Swift ridiculed Gulliver's obsession with the life of Reason, it was Swift's ability to argue a reasoned case which sustained his Irish tracts, his political journalism, and his own life. But Swift was constitutionally as much attracted to the ridicule of platitudes and token gestures as he was to satire of grandiloquent and novel theories, regarding both as empty substitutes for clear thinking, self-knowledge, and the common-sense needs of ordinary living. Of course, Swift has no need to define, least of all to argue, a 'common sense' case. If common sense is that which all reasonable people regard as axiomatic, or at least practical, then defining it would be superfluous and would open up the possibility that the need to explain it necessarily implies its precariousness and its rarity. In the case of critical response to *A Tale of a Tub* Swift's assumption proved mistaken. His intention to 'laugh at those Corruptions in Religion' which '*all* Church of England Men agree in' was interpreted by some of those very churchmen as a dangerous piece of heterodox scepticism. After *A Tale* Swift could not assume that irony was anything else but a dangerous and unpredictable instrument to separate the good from the bad, the follies from the truths. Moreover, the more we read Swift the more we become uncertain as to his own convictions. His own 'positive' loyalties, to the Church of England, to constitutional monarchy, to the tradition of humanist scholarship, and to ideas of order, hierarchy and obedience, are increasingly surrounded with parody, irony, and an undercutting savagery of rhetoric which puts the reader on the defensive. The puzzle of Gulliver's patriotism in particular arises from Swift's own peculiarly paradoxical position as a leader of the Anglo-Irish Establishment, sent to Ireland to maintain English Protestant ascendancy, but convinced that such an ascendancy led directly to the moral and economic rape of the Irish people. Above all other political slogans, patriotism falls an easy victim to party interest, the word itself becoming meaningless as Gulliver praises his country for its exceptional enlightenment and tolerance while the evidence to the contrary is overwhelming.

Swift externalizes such paradoxes. He creates characters like the Modest Proposer and Gulliver who avoid dilemmas by making a choice based on a schematic simplification of reality. Eating babies will both reduce the population and bring increasing economic activity to an overpopulated and economically stagnating Ireland. The corruption endemic in human society may be eradicated if one lives completely separate from the whole species. Happiness is a state of self-deceit. The Tories are right and the Whigs are wrong. The Church of England is the only true religion; everything else is subversive lunacy. All politicians are corrupt and self-seeking. Patriotism is the duty of every virtuous man. Man is a reasonable animal. Vice is ugly, and so on. The difficulty is that there are for Swift no ready answers to be given in language uncontaminated with prejudice, self-interest, and secret motives. The individual self and the public world in which it must live are constantly embattled. Gulliver and the Modest Proposer have become by the end of their narratives completely public men; in the process of devoting themselves to the public benefit they lose their humanity and become instruments of a public policy. In his *Sentiments of a Church-of-England Man, with Respect to Religion and Government* (1711), Swift examined the conflict between the integrity of the individual and the schizophrenia of public performance when reduced to two opposing loyalties:

Whoever hath examined the Conduct and Proceeding of both *Parties* for some Years past, whether in or out of Power, cannot well conceive it possible to go far towards the Extreams of either, without offering some Violence to his Integrity or Understanding. A wise and good Man may indeed be sometimes induced to comply with a Number, whose Opinion he generally approves, although it be perhaps against his own. But this Liberty should be made use of upon very few Occasions, and those of small Importance, and then only with a View of bringing over his own Side another Time to something of greater and more publick Moment. But, to sacrifice the Innocency of a Friend, the Good of our Country, or our own Conscience, to the Humour, or Passion, or Interest, of a Party; plainly shows that either our Heads or our Hearts are not as they should be: Yet this very Practice is the fundamental Law of each Faction among us; as may be obvious to any who will impartially, and without Engagement, be at the Pains to examine their Actions; which, however, is not so easy a Task: For, it seems a Principle in human Nature, to incline one Way more than another, even in Matters where we are wholly unconcerned. *(Prose Works*, II, 1)

Friendship, patriotism, and conscience are casualties of political ambition, and the individual disappears in the public persona. Already, in 1708, when this pamphlet was written, Swift's mind was moving along the lines which would form around the Academy of Political Projectors and the King of Brobdingnag's scathing ridicule of Gulliver's English society. The *Sentiments* concludes with a clear distinction between the priority of individual moral virtue and the inessential expediencies of political mechanisms:

how has this Spirit of Faction mingled it self with the Mass of the People, changed their Nature and Manners, and the very Genius of the Nation? Broke all the Laws of Charity, Neighbourhood, Alliance and Hospitality; destroyed all Ties of Friendship, and divided Families against themselves? And no Wonder it should be so, when in order to find out the Character of a Person; instead of enquiring whether he be a Man of Virtue, Honour, Piety, Wit, good Sense, or Learning; the modern Question is only, Whether he be a *Whig* or *Tory*; under which Terms all good and ill Qualities are included. *(Prose Works*, II, 24)

The implications of this argument have a profound significance for the strategies of Swift's satire. If the integrity of the self is destroyed by the contesting loyalties of public life, then for Swift to argue the case for individual judgement he must show the errors in public ways and in public institutions themselves. Choosing one or another of two polar extremes is playing a literally *self*-destructive game. When Gulliver chooses to emulate the Houyhnhnm life of Reason (in spite of having been ejected from their community), he loses precisely those claims to human sympathy which Swift outlines above: 'Charity, Neighbourhood, Alliance and Hospitality'.

As in Swift's moral philosophy, so in his satire; the central focus is on the self torn by the demands of a public existence in relationship with other and contradictory loyalties. Swift himself slips in and out of his own satire, apparently validating one point of view and in another place ridiculing the same idea, now speaking through a mouthpiece and now catching up his speakers in their own web of words. Such side-stepping charges his satire with a restless and precarious instability, apparently asserting the uncertainty of everything, sabotaging all dogma and at times denying the communicative purpose of language itself.

In the *Sentiments* Swift declared 'a Principle in human Nature, to incline one Way more than another'. Argument by means of polar opposites is a characteristic of his satire as well as a reflection of his view of the human personality. When public myths are in collision with private perception, the result is traumatic. This is particularly clear in some of Swift's poetry, where the split between mind and body is enlarged to grotesque extremes in both cases. In *Cassinus and Peter* (1734) the sophomoric hero worships his mistress through the spectacles of pastoral romance. This literary fiction of the mind is obliterated and replaced by a deep physical loathing when he discovers that '*Caelia, Caelia, Caelia* shits' (l. 118). Like Gulliver, Cassinus lurches from one extreme to another and loses his sanity in the process. If Caelia is not a pastoral nymph she must be a vile body, so Cassinus turns what was once a precious fiction into a contemptible carcass, reducing personality to an excremental act. Such poems by Swift were once thought 'unprintable', but we are unlikely to be shocked merely by four-letter words today. What remains shocking, however, is the prosaic clarity and evenness of tone ('that Simplicity') with which Swift handles the trauma of Cassinus. Sombre denunciations of the sexual attractiveness of women are a commonplace in religious and imaginative literature from St Augustine onwards. Montaigne prescribed a view of the naked female as an antidote to passion:

... although this recipe may proceed from a rather squeamish and frigid disposition, yet it is a wonderful sign of our imperfection that acquaintance and familiarity should make us distasteful to one another. It is not modesty so much as discretion and artfulness that makes our ladies so circumspect in refusing admittance to their boudoir before they are dressed up and painted for public view.

He quotes Lucretius on the same topic:

> *And these our Venuses are 'ware of this,*
> *Wherefore the more are they at pains to hide*
> *All the behind-the-scenes of life from those*
> *Whom they desire to keep in bonds of love.*

Whereas in many animals there is nothing that we do not love, and that does not gratify our senses; so that from their very excrements and discardings we obtain not only dainties to eat, but our richest ornaments and perfumes.

(*Apology for Raimond Sebond, Essays* (1603), II, 12)

There is King Lear's frenzied vision of woman's dual nature:

> *Behold yon simpering dame,*
> *Whose face between her forks presageth snow;*
> *That minces virtue, and does shake the head*
> *To hear of pleasure's name;*

> *The fitchew nor the soiled horse goes to't*
> *With a more riotous appetite.*
> *Down from the waist they are Centaurs,*
> *Though women all above:*
> *But to the girdle do the gods inherit,*
> *Beneath is all the fiends':*
> *There's hell, there's darkness, there is the sulphurous pit,*
> *Burning, scalding, stench, consumption . . .*
>
> (Act IV, scene vi, ll. 121–32)

Burton's *Anatomy of Melancholy* (1621) contains page after page devoted to the absurdity of confusing the literary image of woman with the reality, and the irrational horrors of lust:

To conclude with Chrysostom, 'When thou seest a fair and beautiful person, a brave Bonaroba, a bella donna . . . a comely woman, having bright eyes, a merry countenance, a shining lustre in her look, a pleasant grace, wringing thy soul, and increasing thy concupiscence; bethink with thyself that it is but earth thou lovest, a mere excrement, which so vexeth thee, that thou so admirest, and thy raging soul will be at rest. Take her skin from her face, and thou shalt see all loathsomeness under it, that beauty is a superficial skin and bones, nerves, sinews: suppose her sick, now reviled, hoary-headed, hollow-cheeked, old; within she is full of filthy phlegm, stinking, putrid, excremental stuff: snot and snivel in her nostrils, spittle in her mouth, water in her eyes, what filth in her brains,' &c.

(Part III, Section 2, Mem. 5, Subs. 3)

Nothing that Swift wrote, either in the 'Digression on Madness' (flaying the whore) or in his poetry, has the clinical disgust of Burton's appalling catalogue of female ugliness. Moreover, citing parallels and antecedents for Swift's satire on this subject has little value if its purpose is to 'explain away' Swift's particular treatment as another exercise in a commonplace topic. Burton may deconstruct the beautiful woman in terms far more grotesque and in much greater detail than Swift in order to provide an antidote to lust. But it is characteristic of Swift to look at commonplaces in a completely different way. His angle of vision is both narrower and more intense. Cassinus is not suffering from lust but voyeurism and prurience. He both knows too little and has looked and seen too much. Caelia is the object of his own suppressed bodily shame. His eye is on Caelia, but Swift's eye is on him. In her he sees himself humiliated. Like Gulliver's confrontation with the breast of the Brobdingnagian nursemaid, his horror at the ageing female Struldbrugg, and his second meeting with a Yahoo (IV, 2), Cassinus collapses in shame at the publication of private physical necessities and his own reflection. Urination is thus

> *A Crime that shocks all human Kind;*
> *A Deed unknown to Female Race,*
> *At which the Sun should hide his Face.*   (ll. 68–70)

Caelia's role is as much a product of male stereotyping as the sun is a sign of a male cosmology, and in line 88 the devastated Cassinus quotes a line from *Macbeth* which neatly and unintentionally alludes to his self-implication in Caelia's 'crime', 'Avaunt – ye cannot say 'twas I.' In *The Lady's Dressing Room* there is another voyeur-hero disoriented by literary preconceptions of humanity. Strephon's vision distorts the object he perceives, or, more specifically, his sense of smell determines a view of the feminine personality. But in this case the polarities of body and moral being are seemingly reconciled in a brusque and apparently authorial coda:

> *His foul Imagination links*
> *Each Dame he sees with all her Stinks:*
> *And, if unsav'ry Odours fly,*
> *Conceives a Lady standing by:*
> *All Women his Description fits,*
> *And both Idea's jump like Wits:*
> *By vicious Fancy coupled fast,*
> *And still appearing in Contrast.*
> *I pity wretched* Strephon *blind*
> *To all the Charms of Female Kind;*
> *Should I the Queen of Love refuse,*
> *Because she rose from stinking Ooze?*
> *To him that looks behind the Scene,*
> Satira*'s but some pocky Quean.*
> *When* Celia *in her Glory shows,*
> *If* Strephon *would but stop his Nose;*
> *(Who now so impiously blasphemes*
> *Her Ointments, Daubs, and Paints and Creams,*
> *Her Washes, Slops, and every Clout,*
> *With which he makes so foul a Rout;)*
> *He soon would learn to think like me,*
> *And bless his ravisht Sight to see*
> *Such Order from Confusion sprung,*
> *Such gaudy Tulips rais'd from Dung.*

> (*Poems*, II, 529–30)

When Swift scrutinizes the oldest dichotomy in the world, i.e. that between man and woman, he attacks the literary stereotypes of women as goddesses and disembodied enchanters, not because he believes women are less sinful than men but because men insist on seeing in women something superhuman. His satiric focus is on the eye of the beholders, and they are always men. In *Strephon and Chloe* the former is embarrassed 'How with so high a Nymph he might/Demean himself the Wedding-Night' (ll. 73–4), and is traumatized to discover that a chamberpot is necessary for *both* sexes ('He found her, while the Scent increas'd, /As *mortal* as himself at least' (ll. 185–6)). Again, there is a moral coda, although after the Rabelaisian comedy in the poem it seems flat and homiletic, the merest 'common sense':

> *On Sense and Wit your Passion found,*
> *By Decency cemented round;*
> *Let Prudence with Good Nature strive,*
> *To keep Esteem and Love alive.*
> *Then come old Age whene'er it will,*
> *Your Friendship shall continue still:*
> *And thus a mutual gentle Fire,*
> *Shall never but with Life expire.*

> (*Poems*, II, 593)

A frequent critical response to *Cassinus and Peter, The Lady's Dressing Room, Strephon and Chloe,* and *A Beautiful Young Nymph Going to Bed* is to find the gross physicality of Swift's descriptions offensive and obsessional. It is. Even if we acknowledge that Swift's eye is not on real lovers but on false perceptions, and that such poems are concerned primarily with exploding romantic myths of woman and the absurdity of male bodily self-consciousness, there is nevertheless a visceral specificity which goes far beyond the purposes of romantic parody:

> *How could a Nymph so chaste as* Chloe,
> *With Constitution cold and snowy,*
> *Permit a brutish Man to touch her?*
> *Ev'n Lambs by Instinct fly the Butcher.*
> *Resistance on the Wedding-Night*
> *Is what our Maidens claim by Right:*
> *And,* Chloe, *'tis by all agreed,*
> *Was Maid in Thought, and Word, and Deed,*
> *Yet, some assign a diff'rent Reason;*
> *That* Strephon *chose no proper Season.*   (ll. 151–60)

The implications of that last line have nothing to do with romantic parody; its biological implications cannot be assimilated into a literary game. And yet Swift's whole point is that to exchange a romantic obsession for a definition of the personality entirely construed in terms of its animal functions (excretion, urination, flatulence, even menstruation, etc.) is insane. Disillusionment, not morbidity, is Swift's aim. We need only recall his words to Pope: 'I tell you after all that I do not hate mankind, it is vous autres who hate them because you would have them reasonable animals, and are angry for being disappointed.' The grubby, deluded and patronizing Strephon and Cassinus are writ large in the figure of the myopic Gulliver; just as elements in the human personality which they have repressed are writ large in the figure of the Yahoos.

It may not be pleasant to contemplate female beauty as 'gaudy Tulips rais'd from Dung', the less so because Swift is once again refusing to moderate *either* the beauty *or* the bodily nastiness by using conventional euphemisms. Whether in the mind of the beholder or on the pages of polite literature, euphemism is the fig-leaf which covers inhibition and shame, a device which both conceals and draws attention to physical imperatives. Swift, it should be noticed, eventually puts the fig-leaf back where it was ('On Sense and Wit your Passion found', etc.), because the antidote may be far worse than the original malady:

> *If Decency brings no Supplies,*
> *Opinion falls, and Beauty dies.*
> *To see some radiant Nymph appear*
> *In all her glitt'ring Birth-Day Gear,*
> *You think some Goddess from the Sky*
> *Descended, ready cut and dry:*
> *But, e'er you sell your self to Laughter,*
> *Consider well what may come after;*
> *For fine Ideas vanish fast,*
> *While all the gross and filthy last.* (ll. 225–34)

A lover's imagination is as susceptible to building castles in the air as the philosopher. The conclusion to *The Mechanical Operation of the Spirit* describes their common fate: 'they may branch upwards towards Heaven, but the Root is in the Earth. Too intense a Contemplation is not the Business of Flesh and Blood; it must by the necessary Course of Things, in a little Time, let go its Hold, and fall into *Matter*. Lovers, for the sake of Celestial Converse, are but another sort of *Platonicks*, who pretend to see Stars and Heaven in Ladies Eyes, and to look or think no lower; but the same *Pit* is provided for both; and they seem a perfect Moral to the

Story of that Philosopher, who, while his Thoughts and Eyes were fixed upon the *Constellations*, found himself seduced by his *lower Parts* into a *Ditch*' (*A Tale*, pp. 288–9). Neither heaven nor the ditch are alternatives; they are the extremes between which human nature permanently fluctuates, although the gravitational pull towards the latter is the constant course of Swift's satire. Similarly, in section II of *A Tale*, the sect of tailor-worshippers have determined that 'Man was an Animal compounded of two *Dresses*, the *Natural* and the *Celestial Suit*, which were the Body and the Soul: That the Soul was the outward, and the Body the inward Cloathing . . . separate these two, and you will find the Body to be only a sensless unsavoury Carcass. By all which it is manifest, that the outward Dress must needs be the Soul' (pp. 79–80). Such an argument depends as much upon contempt for the body as it does upon a craving for some 'higher' disembodied reality, and Swift quite clearly savours the perverse intellectual fun of playing with the literal and the figurative imagery of inside/outside, mind/body, reality/ideal. But again, the intention is to expose the *impossibility* of evading the paradoxical nature of man.

In Swift's complimentary poems to Stella and Vanessa the physical imagery is dignified by a concentration on moral and intellectual qualities. The Stella poems in particular stress every kind of relationship except the sexual:

> *Thou* Stella, *wert no longer young,*
> *When first for thee my Harp I strung:*
> *Without one Word of Cupid's Darts,*
> *Of killing Eyes, or bleeding Hearts:*
> *With Friendship and Esteem possesst,*
> *I ne'er admitted Love a Guest.*
> (*To Stella, Who Collected and Transcribed his Poems*, ll. 9–14)

The light raillery, anti-romantic irony and moral bolstering directed at Stella recognize only her ageing and increasing size as physical attributes, compliments only between those who share a precise and mutual understanding of each other's sensibilities. The Stella poems are also in this respect the exact opposite of the poems once termed 'unprintable', where physical dissection, the stripping away of clothes, cosmetics, wigs, perfumes, and so on leaves nothing *but* a degenerate carcass and mutual incomprehension. As with the intellectual satire of the tailor-god, so with the poems to and about women: the error Swift points to is mistaking the surface appearance for anything other than a transient, casual, inessential invention of the mind and its tendency to superimpose the fictional and the imagined on the experienced and the intractable:

> ... with Relation to the Mind or Understanding; 'tis manifest, what mighty Advantages Fiction has over Truth; and the Reason is just at our Elbow; because Imagination can build nobler Scenes, and produce more wonderful Revolutions than Fortune or Nature will be at Expence to furnish ... How fade and insipid do all Objects accost us that are not convey'd in the Vehicle of *Delusion*? How shrunk is every Thing, as it appears in the Glass of Nature? So that if it were not for the Assistance of Artificial *Mediums*, false Lights, refracted Angles, Varnish, and Tinsel; there would be a mighty Level in the Felicity and Enjoyments of Mortal Men ... in most Corporeal Beings, which have fallen under my Cognizance, the *Outside* hath been infinitely preferable to the *In*.
>
> *(Tale, pp. 171–2, 173)*

This argument from Swift's hack author is both slippery and paradoxical. Fiction is equated with Imagination, which is the product of Delusion, whose materials are all hallucinatory. Truth is equated with Nature and Fortune, the universals of all human experience. The dichotomy between Fiction and Nature is man-made, a distortion of reality, but as in the conclusion to *The Lady's Dressing Room*, a *necessary* interface between the real and the imaginary. The argument justifies artifice (cosmetics, superficial attractiveness) as much as it supports the evasions of the intellect in such areas as morality, philosophy, and religion. It suggests that knowing too much is as disconcerting as wilful ignorance, and it implicitly outlines the excruciating dilemma of the satirist himself. The hack author argues for the beauty of surfaces, but in so doing reveals the hypocrisy of the whole exercise. By contrast, Gulliver returns from the land of the Houyhnhnms torn between a memory of 'real' perfection and the inescapable consequences of his own physical bondage:

> My Wife and Family received me with great Surprize and Joy, because they concluded me certainly dead; but I must freely confess, the Sight of them filled me only with Hatred, Disgust and Contempt; and the more, by reflecting on the near Alliance I had to them. For, although since my unfortunate Exile from the *Houyhnhnm* Country, I had compelled myself to tolerate the Sight of *Yahoos*, and to converse with *Don Pedro de Mendez*; yet my Memory and Imaginations were perpetually filled with the Virtues and Ideas of those exalted *Houyhnhnms*. And when I began to consider, that by copulating with one of the *Yahoo*-Species, I had become a Parent of more; it struck me with the utmost Shame, Confusion and Horror.   (IV, 11)

Gulliver is here both the victim of satire and the protagonist in the conflict between Fiction/Imagination and Truth/Nature. Although we cannot for a moment forget that Swift has deliberately trapped Gulliver between two polar opposites (mind and body) which in reality are inseparable, and given him a choice between the two which is itself illusory, there is nevertheless a deep and troubling perception that what Gulliver foolishly fears may indeed be a contemptible folly. When Gulliver says he prefers the company of two horses and the smelly groom to that of his own family he is both the butt of Swift's satire and an envied escapee from the prison of a corrupt sublunary world. Beneath Swift's ridicule there is an image of man's soaring imagination permanently mired in a world in which he is both an exile and a victim. Gulliver's escape is fictional, ludicrous, and impossible. But Swift's imagination has created the possibility.

The challenge that Swift offers his dramatic personae to recognize their own moral and intellectual myopia is never met. Gulliver tells lies to the King of Brobdingnag about his own country and expects the reader's own patriotism to underwrite the deceit:

I artfully eluded many of his Questions; and gave to every Point a more favourable Turn by many Degrees than the Strictness of Truth would allow. For, I have always born that laudable Partiality to my own Country, which *Dionysius Halicarnassensis* with so much Justice recommends to an Historian. I would hide the Frailties and Deformities of my Political Mother, and place her Virtues and Beauties in the most advantageous Light. This was my sincere Endeavour in those many Discourses I had with that Monarch, although it unfortunately failed of Success. (II, 7)

Gulliver offers us the conspirator's role. We are to join knowingly in a club dedicated to the preservation of a patriotic myth. It is as though believing in a desirable fiction will itself make the fiction real; that hypocrisy is better than dissent; and that self-delusion for the sake of a higher cause is a necessary contribution to the New Jerusalem. Samuel Johnson's *The Vanity of Human Wishes* (which includes the line 'And *Swift* expires a Driv'ler and a Show') remorselessly charts the history of human aspiration ending in humiliation, and ends with the conviction that 'celestial Wisdom' has provided the means by which 'the Mind . . . makes the Happiness she does not find'. Gulliver's own exercise in wish-fulfilment is not far from the argument of Swift's doctrinal and non-satirical tract *A Project for the Advancement of Religion and the Reformation of Manners* (1709), written early in his career but nevertheless about the same time as the brilliant and utterly contrasting irony of *An Argument against Abolishing Christianity* (published in 1711). The *Project* proposes that moral reform should be initiated by the monarch choosing candidates for preferment on the basis of Piety and Virtue (the scheme advocated by the King of Brobdingnag). The idea is that if the state ties promotion to moral excellence (or at least loyalty to the established church), then self-interest and politico-ecclesiastical orthodoxy will be the same. Swift also suggests that censorship of the press and an Office of Censors of public morality be established, just in case self-interest is *not* the primary motive for allegiance: 'if Religion were once understood to be the necessary Step to Favour and Preferment; can it be imagined, that any Man would openly offend against it, who had the least Regard for his Reputation or his Fortune?' The psychological basis for this extraordinary proposal is, simply, that 'it is often with Religion as it is with Love; which, by much Dissembling, at last grows real'. The totalitarian implications of the *Project* are crystal clear: if repeated often enough, and if all opposition is strictly suppressed, any officially sponsored dogma may become the received truth. The *argument* of the *Project* excludes the rights of an individual conscience sincerely to choose its own creed and its *rhetoric* provides the reader with no role but one of agreement or rejection. As Ehrenpreis has remarked (II, 277), 'Anyone who tries to combine the *Project* with the *Argument* as existing on the same level of discourse will plunge himself into unnecessary contradictions.' In relation to the satirical discourse of *Gulliver's Travels*, the *Project* seems hardly to come from the same pen. In II, 7, Gulliver's patriotism is exposed as a tissue of lies, self-deception, complacency, insularity, and jingoistic pride. He admits that he has produced a fiction in which he nevertheless believes wholeheartedly. Moreover, his patriotism is the one thing that outlives his contempt for the whole human race; it is the sole survivor of his moral disillusionment at human kind. Four chapters from the end of his book, he praises British colonialism for its exceptional 'Wisdom, Care, and Justice . . . liberal Endowments for the Advancement of Religion . . . Choice of devout and able Pastors to propagate Christianity'. Presumably this is interactive satire, and the reader is intended to discriminate between Gulliver's 'sincerity' and Swift's satirical sub-text which damns by overblown praise. If all the English are Yahoos, they cannot collectively be an example of political and moral enlightenment 'to the whole World'. But in the *Proposal* Swift positively *argues* the case for duplicity:

Hypocrisy is much more eligible than open Infidelity and Vice: It wears the Livery of Religion, it acknowledges her Authority, and is cautious of giving Scandal. Nay, a long continued Disguise, is too great a Constraint upon human Nature, especially an *English* Disposition. Men would leave off their Vices out of meer Weariness, rather than undergo the Toil and Hazard, and perhaps Expence of practising them perpetually in private. And, I believe, it is often with Religion as it is with Love; which, by much Dissembling, at last grows real.

(Prose Works, II, 57)

Having pilloried the sect of tailor-worshippers in *A Tale* for confusing the outside for the inside of things, Swift here declares that the nominal may become the real, that the external trappings of a state religion may become the inner belief, especially if administered by a moral police force. No matter how convinced Swift was that the Church of England was the only true religion, and that Catholicism, dissent and atheism were species of political subversion, it is a strange argument for a priest to support the state religion by such a totalitarian psychology. It would be a difficult task to demonstrate that Swift is being anything other than deadly serious in the *Proposal.* The moral ruthlessness of it indicates a tyranny close to that of the Inquisition.

In the appendix George Orwell wrote for *Nineteen Eighty-Four* the works of Swift (along with those of Shakespeare, Milton, Byron and Dickens) are being translated into Newspeak, the state-controlled language of mind-control, for reasons of 'prestige'. But at least in respect of the *Proposal,* no translation into Newspeak seems necessary. Half-way through the book (in part 2, section 5) the 'last man', Winston Smith, realizes the bliss of ignorance:

... how easy it was to prevent an appearance of orthodoxy while having no grasp whatever of what orthodoxy meant. In a way, the world-view of the Party imposed itself most successfully on people incapable of understanding it. They could be made to accept the most flagrant violations of reality, because they never fully grasped the enormity of what was demanded of them, and were not sufficiently interested in public events to notice what was happening. By lack of understanding they remained sane. They simply swallowed everything, and what they swallowed did them no harm, because it left no residue behind, just as a grain of corn will pass undigested through the body of a bird.

Gulliver, also in his own mind 'the last man' in Europe, digests the rational grain of the Houyhnhnms but allows the grain of patriotism to pass through him without taint. The first engenders misanthropy in him, the second a loyalty to a political system whose unwitting product he is. A desperate need to escape from corrupt humanity is checked by an equal determination to remain the very model of a loyal citizen. Gulliver's dilemma is one that Swift himself knew well in Ireland. In the fictional world of *Gulliver's Travels* Swift could work out some of his deepest loyalties and anxieties, free to ridicule in fantasy worlds the fundamental props of his own political career, and at liberty to scrutinize their unresolved contradictions. It is only by implication that a solution exists to Gulliver's dilemma. As Ehrenpreis has remarked, 'Few readers of *Gulliver's Travels* come away from it feeling that the author has strengthened their devotion to Christianity. So it is fortunate that Swift's real argument lies elsewhere. By locating it not in the soul but in the body, Swift can simply compare the acccount of human nature generally accepted with the data of experience. He can set our theory of morals beside our visible practice. If religion has failed to touch the hearts of men, perhaps they may be moved by elementary shame, by the sight of the abyss between the principles they themselves preach and the corruption of their lives' (Ehrenpreis, I I I, 468). This is undoubtedly what Swift attempts, but it is the effect of his methods which is so profoundly disturbing. It is Swift's ability to give a visceral or concrete reality to abstract ideas or to situations which elicit a strongly *negative* association (of a moral, intellectual, religious or sexual kind) which makes the difference between a homily and a satire. Swift offers an argument which can only be resolved off the page, in the reader's own scrutiny of himself, and in his willingness to compete with Swift's own minimalist expectations.

In crossing from Swift's satirical discourse to his non-satirical discourse we encounter paradoxes and contradictions. Aspects of his radical and questioning scepticism are given free rein in *Gulliver's Travels* and *A Tale* which corrode the edges of certainty and confidence elsewhere. If the *Project* is Swift at his most didactic and constructive, his sermons, one would expect, should contain the strength of conviction associated with the vocation of spiritual mentor and be expressed accordingly in the plain and unadorned style of which we know he approved. Again, it is the context and not the statement alone to which we must pay attention. Swift could not conceive of morality being directed by anything other than a religious conscience, an inner principle which monitored and directed social action. The 'plain honest stuff' from which *On the Testimony of Conscience* is composed (one of only eleven sermons attributed with any certainty to Swift which have been printed) includes statements which are commonplace and common to both sermons *and* satire. Gulliver finds in Houyhnhnmland 'No Scoundrels raised from the Dust upon the Merit of their Vices; or Nobility thrown into it on account of their Virtues' (I V, 10). In his sermon on *Conscience*, Swift remarks that 'although virtuous Men do sometimes accidentally make their Way to Preferment, yet the World is so corrupted, that no Man can reasonably hope to be rewarded in it, meerly upon account of his Virtue' (*Prose*

93

Works, IX, 155). Gulliver takes on the tone and moral duties of the preacher, but he is denied the ultimate sanction of the sacerdotal office. In the sermon Swift goes on to say:

> ... the Fear of Punishment in this Life will preserve Men from very few Vices, since some of the blackest and basest do often prove the surest Steps to Favour; such as Ingratitude, Hypocrisy, Treachery, Malice, Subornation, Atheism, and many more which human Laws do little concern themselves about. But when Conscience placeth before us the Hopes of everlasting Happiness, and the Fears of everlasting Misery, as the Reward and Punishment of our good or evil Actions, our Reason can find no way to avoid the Force of such an Argument, otherwise than by running into Infidelity ... a Religious Conscience is the only true solid Foundation upon which Virtue can be built ... (*Prose Works,* IX, 155, 156)

In theological terms Swift accepts the corruption of the world as its permanent characteristic, noting that if virtue is rewarded in this world it is by chance. The worst moral crimes go unpunished. In the context of a sermon such bleak judgements slip by with little emotional charge, and without the least whiff of irony or inflaming rhetoric. Corruption and injustice are the social realities against which the arguments of a Christian conscience must stand. The ameliorations of justice are realities only in the next world, although their distribution depends upon the conduct of the individual in *this* world. Gulliver, by contrast, is denied such consolation. Like Sir Thomas More's Stoics (*Utopia,* I, 39), who make 'no distinction in the gravity of crimes' and who 'consider purse-snatching equal to homicide', Gulliver's seemingly endless and undiscriminating list of human vice and folly in IV, 10 tells only one side of the story. There is no need to travel round the world in order to 'discover' that humanity is a bad lot. There is as much moral disillusionment in Swift's single sermon as in the whole of *Gulliver's Travels,* but Gulliver sees the solution to human depravity in an entirely *secular* context. We recall that Gulliver listens to the Houyhnhnms' conversations with the zeal of a new convert: 'Their Subjects are generally on Friendship and Benevolence; on Order and Oeconomy; sometimes upon the visible Operations of Nature, or Ancient Traditions; upon the Bounds and Limits of Virtue; upon the unerring Rules of Reason' (IV, 10). In his sermon Swift will not consider the possibility that a virtuous life can exist apart from religious principles. He asks:

> If Conscience be so sure a Director to us Christians in the Conduct of our Lives, how cometh it to pass, that the ancient Heathens, who had no other Lights but those of Nature and Reason, should so far exceed us in all manner of Virtue, as plainly appears by many Examples they have left on record? (IX, 155)

The answer to this is not that the 'ancient Heathens' were naturally good (Swift can hardly argue that religious convictions are independent of a morally admirable society), but that they educated their children better, instilled into them a love of their country, and subscribed to a doctrine of rewards and punishments after death. In other words, they were unenlightened Christians in all but name, practising all the moral virtues of the Houyhnhnms but in the context of a divine judgement. Gulliver, by contrast, loathes his children, espouses a patriotism which Swift undercuts as jingoistic tunnel vision, and takes on the self-appointed task of judge and censor to the universe through the flimsy vehicle of a popular and 'low-brow' travel-book. Gulliver's burning moral zeal is not so much the object of Swift's satire, but his naive expectation that reading a single book written by a man of quite ordinary competence will change the world most certainly is.

This classic text of children's literature owes its status not only to the delightful comedy of pigmies and giants, its fantastic invention and amazing discoveries: it also ridicules the posturing world of adulthood through the childlike vision of a naive observer. In the fourth voyage Gulliver grows out of his humanity, and what he sees reflected in the world of the Yahoos and Houyhnhnms drives him back to moral adolescence, to an orphan's idea of adulthood as an institutional thing, responsible but not responsive, authoritarian without love, dependable but emotionally neutral. The final absurdity of Gulliver is that every previous voyage has instructed him in the folly of high expectations and yet he persists, one man alone, in dreaming of a rational utopia none but himself may inhabit. Without recourse to metaphysical consolations, Gulliver is trapped in a private hell. He has swallowed the Houyhnhnm orthodoxy and wakes to find that the life of Reason is a false and inadequate solution to the *human* situation. He directs his Friendship and Benevolence towards actual horses, not to his fellow men. His logic is unimpeachable, but his decision is absurd.

6 'A manifest Dilemma': the Mind and the Book

In section VIII of *A Tale of a Tub* Swift's hack author generates the following psychological explanation of religious fanaticism. As is frequently the case in Swift's satire, the local reference is far outstripped by much larger implications:

... whereas the Mind of Man, when he gives the Spur and Bridle to his Thoughts, doth never stop, but naturally sallies out into both extreams of High and Low, of Good and Evil; His first Flight of Fancy, commonly transports Him to Idea's of what is most Perfect, finished, and exalted; till having soared out of his own Reach and Sight, not well perceiving how near the Frontiers of Height and Depth, border upon each other; With the same Course and Wing, he falls down plumb into the lowest Bottom of Things; like one who travels the *East* into the *West*; or like a strait Line drawn by its own Length into a Circle. Whether a Tincture of Malice in our Natures, makes us fond of furnishing every bright Idea with its Reverse; Or, whether Reason reflecting upon the Sum of Things, can, like the Sun, serve only to enlighten one half of the Globe, leaving the other half, by Necessity, under Shade and Darkness: Or, whether Fancy, flying up to the imagination of what is Highest and Best, becomes over-shot, and spent, and weary, and suddenly falls like a dead Bird of Paradise, to the Ground. Or, whether after these *Metaphysical* Conjectures, I have not entirely missed the true Reason; The Proposition, however, which hath stood me in so much Circumstance, is altògether true; That, as the most unciviliz'd Parts of Mankind, have some way or other, climbed up into the Conception of a *God*, or Supream Power, so they have seldom forgot to provide their Fears with certain ghastly Notions, which instead of better, have served them pretty tolerably for a *Devil*. And this Proceeding seems to be natural enough; For it is with Men, whose Imaginations are lifted up very high, after the same Rate, as with those, whose Bodies are so; that, as they are delighted with the Advantage of a nearer Contemplation upwards, so they are equally terrified with the dismal Prospect of the Precipice below.

(*Tale*, pp. 157–8)

Twenty-two years later the same metaphors of travel, flight, frontiers and compass points are used again, but with greater physical reality, in *Gulliver's Travels*. The ideas in this passage, and their arrangement into pairs of opposites, map the permanent Swiftian fascination for entrapment and escape. On the one hand there is High, Good, East, straight, Sun, Reason, soaring, Imagination, God, Up, and the 'Perfect, finished, exalted'. On the other there is Low, Evil, West, circle, Shade, Fancy/Imagination, 'falls like a dead Bird', Reason, the Devil, Down, 'the lowest Bottom of Things'. The passage provides an essential grammar of Swift's satirical rhetoric. But in addition to this pattern of dichotomies between which the human mind swings in a permanent state of flux, there is a radical perception that the whole neat arrangement may be a delusion, a fiction of the mind. What seem to be extremes may meet in identity: God may be the Devil, and the Devil may be God. Of course, Swift disclaims this as the desperate and crazy incompetence of a hack writer ('whether after these *Metaphysical* Conjectures, I have not entirely missed the true Reason'), but the ironical evasion manages to make the point at the very moment it seems to deny it. We are invited to dismiss such 'Metaphysical Conjectures' as useless, far above the competence of man's intellect, paradoxical, and the product of a deranged mind. Yet, as in the 'Digression on Madness', it is a mistake to dismiss such passages as the ravings of a madman. The mental energy of such a passage impresses us with its prodigality of invention, its rapid movement from one conceit-like analogy to another, and it fascinates us because it is itself an example of its own argument. In context, Swift is satirizing the Aeolists, a composite allegory of religious fanaticism. The Aeolists believe 'the Original Cause of all Things to be *Wind*, from which Principle this whole Universe was at first produced, and into which it must at last be resolved; that the same Breath which had kindled, and blew *up* the Flame of Nature, should one Day blow it *out*' (*Tale*, p. 150). Thus religious inspiration, learning, flatulence, belching and eructation are all derived from the intake or expulsion of wind, either into or from the upper or the lower faculties:

First, it is generally affirmed, or confess'd that Learning *puffeth Men up*: And Secondly, they proved it by the following Syllogism; *Words are but Wind*; *and Learning is nothing but Words*; Ergo, *Learning is nothing but Wind*.

(*Tale*, p. 153)

One could go a long way in interpreting Swift's whole satirical output in terms of inflation and deflation, or, in psychoanalytical terms, sublimation and repression. Strephon and Cassinus both discover in their respective goddesses an element in their own personality which they have repressed; the Modest Proposer raises his shocked sight above the oppressive physical squalor of Dublin poverty to the elegant and abstract systems of quantitative mathematics; the scientists of Laputa are caught between the decaying physical world and the abstract delights of intellectual speculation, 'one of their Eyes turned inward, and the other directly up to the Zenith' (III, 2); the cryptographers in the School of

Political Projectors analyse the contents of a close-stool to find out secret plots and covert intentions in high places; Gulliver sublimates the single faculty of Reason and represses the animal in his nature; the imaginative logic of the first two voyages as a whole is based on relativities of size, which for a time rearrange the conventional relationships between body and mind; and, most remarkable of all, *The Mechanical Operation of the Spirit* illustrates a theory that all intellectual activity is the product of physical repression:

> ... if this Plant has found a Root in the Fields of *Empire*, and of *Knowledge*, it has fixt deeper, and spread yet farther upon *Holy Ground*. Wherein, though it hath pass'd under the general Name of *Enthusiasm*, and perhaps arisen from the same Original, yet hath it produced certain Branches of a very different Nature, however often mistaken for each other. The Word in its universal Acceptation, may be defined, *A lifting up of the Soul or its Faculties above Matter.* This Description will hold good in general; but I am only to understand it, as applied to *Religion;* wherein there are three general Ways of ejaculating the Soul, or transporting it beyond the Sphere of Matter. The first, is the immediate Act of God, and is called, *Prophecy* or *Inspiration.* The second, is the immediate Act of the Devil, and is termed *Possession.* The third, is the product of natural Causes, the effect of strong Imagination, Spleen, violent Anger, Fear, Grief, Pain, and the like ... the fourth Method of *Religious Enthusiasm*, or launching out the Soul, as it is purely an Effect of Artifice and *Mechanick Operation*, has been sparingly handled, or not at all, by any Writer ... *(Tale*, pp. 266–7)

In ridiculing the fanatics, Swift also calls into question the whole basis of spiritual experience. The specific targets – Puritanism, Irish Nonconformism, '*English* Enthusiastic Preachers', Dutch Anabaptists, German Lutherans, Quakers, and other dissenting sects – are all swallowed up in a general theory of inspiration caused by sexual sublimation (the first stage of which is sexual repression). The exuberant parody begins to feed off all religion, including the Anglicanism which Swift is implicitly defending, as soon as the meddlesome mind of man turns from unquestioning assent to inquisitive analysis. It seems that religious experience can only be defined in terms which diminish and even ridicule its very essence. Language itself is rooted in a physical world, and its earthbound *meta*-physical powers are limited by its human exponents. A circular argument is Swift's characteristic image of the human dilemma. After a short flight, the mind drops to earth like a dead bird of paradise; inspiration may be either celestial or satanic; whatever man creates bears the imprint of his failure.

The power of Swift's writing is directed at denying the possibility of answers, but his subject is always the confrontation of the individual mind with its own inquiring nature. We are nearer to the Yahoo in terms of our physical imprisonment, but we share the intellectual nature of the Houyhnhnm. As Alexander Pope put it in the *Essay on Man*, man 'hangs between; in doubt to deem himself a God, or Beast; / In doubt his Mind or Body to Prefer'. Swift and Pope may agree, but stylistically they could not be more apart from each other. Whereas the poet makes dazzlingly precise and elegantly balanced couplets from such paradoxes, Swift imitates through parody the tortuous circularities of man's 'Chaos of Thought and Passion, all confus'd'. The shape of a sentence and the undulations of syntax (exemplified in both the passages quoted above) suggest how close Swift's own conviction of disorder and instability is to the desperate caricatures he offers up to ridicule. The mind of a crazy or dishonest narrator provides Swift with the freedom to express both the farce and the tragedy of existence. The former elicits serious comedy, the prospect that a zany theory pushed far enough will uncover radical instabilities in everything, and the latter elicits the painful recognition that idealism is itself ridiculous. The style generates an intense reaction like a piece of phosphorus in water, consuming itself in a short blaze of intense energy, but in so doing sets up a chain reaction which overflows from the topical to the general. Although this fierce energy is most conspicuous in its 'negative' deployment in satire, it is also a feature of Swift's more detailed political writing. *The Drapier's Letters* had a specific and 'local' purpose to mobilize Irish opposition to the imposition of Wood's copper coinage. The particular process of exposing Wood's scheme rests, however, on a general theory of political and civil liberties, a concept of the natural inherent rights of man, and a view of Irish nationalism a century ahead of its time which was to have profound effects for other English colonies at the end of the century. An episode in the fifth of the *Letters*, to the Lord Chancellor of Ireland, Baron Brodrick of Midleton, shows how Swift steers his way through language discredited by public misuse in order to establish a set of positive credentials:

I believe you will please to allow me two Propositions: First, that we are a most loyal People; and, Secondly, that we are a free People, in the common Acceptation of that Word applied to a Subject under a limited Monarch. I know very well, that you and I did many Years ago in Discourse differ much, in the Presence of Lord *Wharton*, about the Meaning of that Word *Liberty*, with Relation to *Ireland*. But if you will not allow us to be a free People; there is only another Appellation left; which, I doubt, my Lord Chief Justice *Whitshed* would call me to an Account for, if I ventured to bestow: For, I observed, and shall never forget upon what Occasion, the Device upon his Coach to be *Libertas & natale Solum*; at the very

99

Point of Time when he was sitting in his Court, and perjuring himself to betray both. (*Prose Works*, X, 100–101)

Lord Chief Justice William Whitshed had presided over the trial of Edward Waters, the printer of Swift's *Proposal for the Universal Use of Irish Manufacture* (1720). Waters was found not guilty by the jury, but Whitshed sent them back nine times and held them for eleven hours. Whitshed also presided at the trial of *The Drapier's Letters'* printer, Harding, with a similar result. At some stage Swift noticed the motto painted on Whitshed's coach. In the above passage, and in a poem on the motto (*Poems*, I, 347–9), Swift savours the contradiction between principle and practice, and between a liberty for which a man risks his ears and freedom and a liberty to tyrannize over others. Liberty, a fine and ambiguous idea, and one to which Swift himself was entirely dedicated in Ireland, seemed to be as much debased in Whitshed's hands as the coinage Ireland was being coerced into accepting. The words a man lives by can often be turned against him:

> LIBERTAS & natale Solum;
> *Fine Words; I wonder where you stole 'um.*
> *Could nothing but thy chief Reproach,*
> *Serve for a Motto on thy Coach?*
> *But, let me now the Words translate:*
> Natale Solum: *My Estate:*
> *My dear Estate, how well I love it;*
> *My Tenants, if you doubt, will prove it:*
> *They swear I am so kind and good,*
> *I hug them till I squeeze their Blood.*
>
> LIBERTAS *bears a large Import;*
> *First; how to swagger in a Court;*
> *And, secondly, to shew my Fury*
> *Against an uncomplying Jury:*
> *And, Thirdly; 'tis a new Invention*
> *To favour* Wood *and keep my Pension:*
> *And, Fourthly; 'tis to play an odd Trick,*
> *Get the Great Seal, and turn out* Brod'rick.
> *And, Fifthly; you know whom I mean,*
> *To humble that vexatious Dean.* (ll. 1–20)

Whitshed, it seems, makes an emblem of Liberty but a habit of repression: he is portrayed as a feudal tyrant keeping his tenant-inferiors subjected and an unprincipled self-seeker currying favour with the influential for the purpose of personal advancement. There is one law for the rich and powerful, and there is licence of another kind for those in high office. Underneath the lampoon, of course, there is the more fundamental battle for freedom of expression, with Swift as champion and his printers as victims, and it is significant that Swift's imagination is triggered again by the combination of political repression and linguistic sublimation of 'low' motives. Language can be used as a device to erect *'Edifices in the Air'* with as much intention to control as to communicate, just as the Flying Island of Laputa hovers over its enemy territory, blocking out enlightenment from the sun.

Swift composed and published *The Drapier's Letters* during the writing of *Gulliver's Travels*. At the end of January 1724, in the middle of the Wood's Ha'pence controversy, Swift had finished the fourth voyage and was 'in the flying island'. Swift's attacks on William Wood and Justice Whitshed are occasional, 'local' and historically limited episodes in his satirical output. But this does not mean that Swift radically altered his rhetoric when dealing with the general or impersonal. His imagination remains poised between the particular and the mythic, prone to construct fable and allegory out of the accident of a name, just as Gulliver and his travel-book are perched uneasily between verisimilitude and fantasy, and between the 'real' world of autobiographical writing and the subterranean purposes of a fictional satire on man in general. Thus Wood is described in *Some Observations . . . relating to Wood's Half-pence* (1724) as Goliath to Swift's David:

I may say for *Wood*'s Honour, as well as my own, that he resembles *Goliah* in many Circumstances, very applicable to the present Purpose: for Goliah had a Helmet of BRASS *upon his Head, and he was armed with a Coat of Mail, and the Weight of the Coat was five Thousand Shekles of* BRASS*, and he had Greaves of* BRASS *upon his Legs, and a Target of* BRASS *between his Shoulders.* In short, he was like Mr *Wood*, all over BRASS; and *he defied the Armies of the living God.*   (*Prose Works*, X, 48)

The comic-epic machinery promotes Wood as a modern pretender, an overblown parodic image of the Philistine giant, and Swift's armies (also mocked by this ragged metaphor) are the Irish themselves, led by their Anglican Drapier-Dean. We all know what happened to Goliath; but Swift cannot use the confident sweep of parallel history in the way that Dryden used the device in, say, *Absalom and Achitophel*, where he puts the threat from Shaftesbury-Achitophel into a mock-heroic context of a biblical rebellion that failed, thereby prejudging history. On 25 August

1724, there was no telling how the Wood controversy would turn out. But more important than this, Swift shies away from commitment to any heroic or 'literary' role for himself. The disguise he chooses to adopt is not lifted *above* the conflict but deep inside it. His mouthpiece is created from the very classes to which he would have little personal loyalty or intimacy of feeling, the middle-class tradesman, and with whom he would share few intellectual interests. As Herbert Davis once pointed out, though without marking the consequences of the parallel, M.B. Drapier has much in common with Lemuel Gulliver, whose 'Birth was of the lower Sort, having been born of plain, honest Parents, who were just able to give me a tolerable Education' (IV, 6). Neither is as straightforward as he seems; neither can reflect more than a part of Swift's own personality, but both adopt a self-apologetic confidence based on a conviction that their arguments are invincible. We know that both characters are aspects of Swift, devices by which his satirical imagination may be given freer licence than was possible for the Dean of St Patrick's Cathedral, but in both characters we see Swift reaching past the partial fiction to stress the urgency of the message. In his *Letter to Mr Harding the Printer*, M.B. writes

that you are much to blame. Several Hundred Persons have enquired at your House, for my *Letter to the Shop-Keepers*, &c. and you had none to sell them. Pray keep your self provided with that Letter, and with this; you have got very well by the former; but I did not then write for your Sake, any more than I do now. Pray advertise both in every News-Paper; and let it not be your Fault or mine, if our Countrymen will not take Warning. I desire you, likewise, to sell them as cheap as you can.   (*Prose Works*, X , 24)

Swift demanded and received only £200 for *Gulliver's Travels*. We do not know how much Gulliver would have asked for his reforming work. But whereas M.B. complains about his printer's dilatoriness in propagating his important work, Gulliver berates his publisher for persuading him to publish in the first place. M.B.'s tracts are selling like hot cakes, but Gulliver's message seems to have dissipated into thin air and a babble of misprints and misinterpretation:

for instead of seeing a full Stop put to all Abuses and Corruptions, at least in this little Island, as I had Reason to expect: Behold, after above six Months Warning, I cannot learn that my Book hath produced one single Effect according to mine Intentions: I desired you would let me know by a Letter, when Party and Faction were extinguished; Judges learned and upright; Pleaders honest and modest, with some Tincture of Common Sense; and *Smithfield* blazing with Pyramids of Law-

Books; the young Nobility's Education entirely changed; the Physicians banished; the Female *Yahoos* abounding in Virtue, Honour, Truth and good Sense: Courts and Levees of great Ministers thoroughly weeded and swept; Wit, Merit and Learning rewarded; *all Disgracers of the Press in Prose and Verse, condemned to eat nothing but their own Cotten, and quench their Thirst with their own Ink*. These, and a thousand other Reformations, I firmly counted upon by your Encouragement; as indeed they were plainly deducible from the Precepts delivered in my Book. And, it must be owned, that seven Months were a sufficient Time to correct every Vice and Folly to which *Yahoos* are subject; if their Natures had been capable of the least Disposition to Virtue or Wisdom: Yet so far have you been from answering mine Expectations in any of your Letters; that on the contrary, you are loading our Carrier every Week with Libels, and Keys, and Reflections, and Memoirs, and Second Parts; wherein I see myself accused of reflecting upon great States-folk; of degrading human Nature, (for so they still have the Confidence to stile it) and of abusing the Female Sex. I find likewise, that the Writers of those Bundles are not agreed among themselves; *for some of them will not allow me to be the Author of mine own Travels; and others make me Author of Books to which I am wholly a Stranger*.

('Letter to Sympson'; italics added)

Gulliver's private vision, created by the totalitarian Houyhnhnms, has been fragmented by public reception among human kind; the mad wholeness of his moral recipe has been disintegrated by interpreters who have used his discourse as a platform for their own. Far from putting an end to corruption, Gulliver's book has simply generated more books, and Gulliver himself is being submerged in an uncontrollable world of print. Swift is playing some complex games here. He is quite clearly sporting with the pseudonymity of the book, mocking Gulliver's absurdly self-righteous confidence in a single universal vision, and crowding Gulliver's notion of reparable corruption with an assumption that any reasonable man would realize that human corruption is endemic, not casual. The quarrelsome rage expressed by Gulliver is also Swift's own. Gulliver is furious that both his authenticity and his authorship are being questioned and would dearly wish to see his enemies literally eat their own words. At this point Gulliver's rage and his creator's satiric purposes neatly coincide, for if one were looking for a single definition of Swift's theory of parody there would be none more apposite than the idea of the book as a consumable object.

Parody consumes its model and books are no more than the public expression of an individual ego. The contentiousness about which Gulliver complains in human society – the wrangling disputations about self-evident truths – has been carried over from human psychology into the world of print. With Swift's powerfully objectifying imagination,

Gulliver's own book has joined the battle of the books. The King of Brobdingnag had only a thousand books in his library, and the Houyhnhnms had 'not the least Idea of Books or Literature' (IV, 3); they are exponents of oral teaching and traditional wisdom. They had no word for 'Opinion' and find Reason an infallible guide to immediately recognizable truth. Gulliver speculates to himself about the havoc such a principle would cause in the libraries of Europe and reflects upon the wisdom of Plato's conviction that studying moral philosophy, or ethics, is better than determining between opinions and beliefs. *The Battle of the Books* shows how early Swift's mind turned on this problem. The brain surgery proposed as an antidote to party strife in *Gulliver's Travels*, III, 6, is anticipated in *The Battle* by the feud between traditional classics such as Aristotle and Plato and 'Books of Controversy': 'I advised, that the Champions of each side should be coupled together, or otherwise mixt, that like the blending of contrary Poysons, their Malignity might be employ'd among themselves' (*Tale*, p. 224). Gulliver's despair at 'Controversies, Wranglings, Disputes, and Positiveness in false or dubious Propositions' (IV, 8) is a pale shadow compared with Swift's earlier image of the goddess Criticism, a concentrated allegory of the Modern intellectual vices of solipsism and intellectual incest:

She dwelt on the Top of a snowy Mountain in *Nova Zembla*; there *Momus* found her extended in her Den, upon the Spoils of numberless Volumes half devoured. At her right Hand sat *Ignorance*, her Father and Husband, blind with Age; at her left, *Pride* her Mother, dressing her up in the Scraps of Paper herself had torn. There, was *Opinion* her Sister, light of Foot, hoodwinkt, and headstrong, yet giddy and perpetually turning. About her play'd her Children, *Noise* and *Impudence*, *Dullness* and *Vanity, Positiveness, Pedantry,* and *Ill-Manners* . . . Her Eyes turned inward, as if she lookt only upon herself: Her Diet was the overflowing of her own *Gall*: Her *Spleen* was so large, as to stand prominent like a Dug of the first Rate, nor wanted Excrescensies in form of Teats, at which a Crew of ugly Monsters were greedily sucking; and, what is wonderful to conceive, the bulk of Spleen encreased faster than the Sucking could diminish it.   (*Tale*, p. 240)

More than twenty years before the *Travels* Swift was outlining in a *single* image of Modern Criticism the complex and separated components of the four voyages. It is as though interpretation itself is an aspect of sin. Criticism spawns children nurtured on poison, and as repellent as the Yahoos: the traditional oral wisdom of the Houyhnhnms is communicated by word of mouth, not in writing. Like critics, the Yahoos fight among themselves: the Houyhnhnms occupy a serene world of communally recognized truths. Disputation is unknown to them; even if it were, it would probably be regarded as bad form. Proliferation of books devoted to interpretation and controversy seems to argue a genetic disease in the city of literature. Monsters are the result. In Houyhnhnmland, by contrast, there is the opposite link between uniform consensus and common beliefs and a racial policy determined solely by eugenic considerations: only the best stock will thrive. The Goddess Criticism has a vivid and bestial energy shared only by the Yahoos. The spawning of books threatens the purity of 'original' truth, children grow wiser than their parents, beaux become politicians, schoolboys turn judges of philosophy, and *'Coffee-House Wits instinct by Me, can correct an Author's Style, and display his Minutest Errors, without understanding a Syllable of his Matter or his Language'* (*Tale*, p. 241).

Swift's satire on the corruptions of Modern learning in *The Battle of the Books* was energized by a defence of Sir William Temple's aristocratic and therefore hierarchical cultural loyalties. These loyalties were hostile to and also an easy victim of the new rigour in mathematics, textual scholarship, and the experimental sciences. To become one of the new 'experts' meant losing the *sprezzatura* of the gentleman, that elegant ease of manner which condoned blunders of scholarship for the sake of civilized performance in the preservation of amateur intellectualism. It is no accident that Swift and Pope (in *The Dunciad*) see an exclusive culture assailed by crowds, swarms, plagues, as well as footmen, lackeys, stewards and social parvenus. Fear of the mob was no literary neurosis but a social consequence of eighteenth-century English urban life, as the Sacheverell and Gordon riots clearly indicate. Their sense of belonging to a besieged cultural minority threatened by social contamination from the lower classes and from critics is a complex reaction to a changing culture (one sign of which was the emergence of the *déclassé* form of the novel, for which there was neither an inherited form nor place in neo-classical literary theory). Gulliver transmits his fear of humanity in the mass by rejecting it. He also reflects in the letter to Sympson an alienation caused by the very process of book production. Gulliver cannot know his audience; his book has become public property, and when he sees its printed form he barely recognizes it. On his deathbed Pope thought of himself as 'like Socrates, distributing my morality among my friends', but Gulliver's moral wisdom has been mangled by a careless printer and by ignorant, hostile and unteachable Yahoos.

Being misunderstood was a fact of Swift's own career, and a permanently damaging one. When he wrote *The Author upon Himself* in 1714 Swift was doubtless reflecting not only on the collapse of the Harley–

Bolingbroke ministry but also on the consequent eclipse of his own career. The shadow had been cast ten years earlier, with the publication of *A Tale of a Tub*:

> Swift had the Sin of Wit no venial Crime;
> Nay, 'twas affirm'd, he sometimes dealt in Rhime:
> Honour, and Mirth, had Place in all he writ:
> He reconcil'd Divinity and Wit.
> He mov'd, and bow'd, and talk't with too much Grace;
> Nor shew'd the Parson in his Gait or Face.

(*Poems*, I, 193–4)

The life of a Wit was warfare upon earth, and '*Ink* is the great missive Weapon, in all Battels of the *Learned*' (*Tale*, p. 221). One disease of the Modern world races past even the worst of the seven deadly sins:

> All Human Race wou'd fain be Wits,
> And Millions miss, for one that hits.
> Young's universal Passion, Pride,
> Was never known to spread so wide.

(*On Poetry: A Rhapsody*, 1733: *Poems*, II, 640)

In the second paragraph of *The Battle of the Books* Swift describes the warfare in print as a stand-off, a resolution of opposition by means of slogans,

as the *Grecians*, after an Engagement, when they could not *agree* about the Victory, were wont to set up Trophies on both sides, the beaten Party being content to be at the same Expence, to keep it self in Countenance (A laudable and antient Custom, happily reviv'd of late, in the Art of War) so the *Learned*, after a sharp and bloody Dispute, do on both sides hang out their Trophies too, which-ever comes by the worst. These Trophies have largely inscribed on them the Merits of the Cause; a full impartial Account of such a Battel, and how the Victory fell clearly to the Party that set them up. They are known to the World under several Names; as *Disputes, Arguments, Rejoynders, Brief Considerations, Answers, Replies, Remarks, Reflexions, Objections, Confutations,* ... *Books of Controversie.* (*Tale*, pp. 221–2)

Gulliver's last words come first, in the letter to Sympson, and their purpose is to cut the ground from under all attempts to *dispute* the reality of his experiences, to 'think my Book of Travels a meer Fiction out of mine own Brain ... that the *Houyhnhnms* and *Yahoos* have no more Existence than the Inhabitants of *Utopia*'. His readers are left to squabble about literary–critical questions, and Gulliver departs gloomily convinced that the whole dispute simply demonstrates that mankind has once again avoided its own reflection. Gulliver is convinced that 'Truth immediately strikes every Reader with Conviction', however, and his letter assumes the co-existence of 'judicious and candid Readers' and a generality of obtuse idiots who will certainly misconstrue his meaning. The ambiguity of course is generated because there are two voices speaking here, Gulliver's and Swift's. The former's *veracity* is undercut by the latter's signal that *Utopia* is indeed a framework inside which this latter-day Hythloday brings back news from nowhere. But Gulliver is also placed in the unenviable position of a prophet to whom nobody will listen, and of a preacher compromised by idealistic aims and the impossibility of correct interpretation. The mysteries of religion are no less inscrutable to man than the nature of man himself. Swift's *Letters to a Young Gentleman, Lately Entered into Holy Orders* (1721) spells out the limits of explanation and more significantly, in view of what *Gulliver's Travels* was soon to achieve, the communicative *superiority* of allegorical fiction over an abstract philosophical analysis:

> I have been better entertained, and more informed by a Chapter in the *Pilgrim's Progress*, than by a long Discourse upon the *Will* and the *Intellect*, and *simple* or *complex Ideas* . . .
>   I do not find that you are any where directed in the Canons, or Articles, to attempt explaining the Mysteries of the Christian Religion. And, indeed, since Providence intended there should be Mysteries; I do not see how it can be agreeable to *Piety*, *Orthodoxy*, or *good Sense*, to go about such a Work. For, to me there seems to be a manifest Dilemma in the Case: If you explain them, they are Mysteries no longer; if you fail, you have laboured to no Purpose . . . Neither is it strange, that there should be Mysteries in Divinity, *as well as in the commonest Operations of Nature*.   (*Prose Works*, IX, p. 77)

Thus Gulliver's protestations about the truthfulness of his experiences simply reinforce their fictionality. He protests about the medium and Swift thereby puts up a smoke-screen for the literal-minded, a floating tub designed to distract the whale of criticism while the satirical message proceeds on its way. Gulliver's pride in authorship is frustrated by the reception of his book: it is also satirized by Swift because Gulliver is himself a fiction desperately struggling to assert his reality. Among Swift's own 'judicious and candid Readers', Pope kept up the fictional delight in a series of poems, including Mrs Gulliver's lament about his strange preference for the company of horses. To some extent, therefore, Swift's response to Gulliver's revelations parallels the more obvious textual undercutting of the hack author of *A Tale of a Tub* (the gaps in the manuscript, the confession of madness, etc.). But Swift had no wish to provide the reader with the chance to patronize Gulliver, nor with the escape route of self-exculpation. Gulliver's misanthropy is universal; nobody is guiltless because all readers are human, and Swift has finally created a mirror for all mankind, including himself. In the letter to Sympson Gulliver has become the reader of his own text, Swift having relinquished all 'authorial' control to the mechanical responsibility of the printing process.

Gulliver's Travels is not a novel. Its purposes are far too many to be served by the depiction of a psychological realism and a single viewpoint. It is a mixed satire of ideas, held together by a double perspective. It does not imitate reality, it distorts it, recreating imagined fictions in place of it and then scrutinizing the actual process whereby the distortions are formed. Even so, the rhetorical and interpretative problems to which the *Travels* gives rise are not unrelated to those of the emerging novel. Swift had, after all, anticipated the novel's rise in *A Tale of a Tub*, sabotaging the narrative ego, putting up the notion of form only to let it tumble around the ears of its creator, and splitting apart the world of the imagination from the world of actuality. Swift's narrators are each confronted with the desperate difficulty of defining their reading audience; each constructs a fiction as a means of teaching us something about the real world; *their* monocular vision exists in parallel with, and often separate from, *Swift's* binocular focus. Broadly speaking, Swift's satirical texts are parasites drawing their form and structure from pre-existing texts – the learned book, the travel-book, the economic tract, the pastoral poem, the religious tract. Above all else, *A Tale of a Tub* parodies the nature of Modern writing by submerging content in form, exhibiting the failure of the author to say anything new or valuable, but at the same time showing that even the insights of a lunatic may reveal awkward truth. Like Samuel Beckett, Swift shows that the fictions we live by are neither dispensable nor altogether absurd. The central feature of Swift's satire is its dramatic ambiguity: behind the voice of the posturing author there is the acerbic wit of Swift himself. We hear them both at the same time, just as Swift himself thought of books as speaking voices: 'When I am reading a Book, whether wise or silly, it seemeth to me to be alive and talking to me' (*Prose Works*, IV, 253). Swift is the script-writer, performer, audience, and critic, daring us to believe half of his fiction.

7 Conclusion

The kind of scepticism we bring to bear on Swift's writing is perhaps the most positive single effect of his satire. We learn to distrust Swift's narrators and to withhold our assent from their arguments because their confidence in a single viewpoint topples over into a revelation of private obsession. Nothing is to be taken at face value because the faces that Swift turns to us are themselves but masks for a powerful and unstable individual ego. Their pose of representativeness, their patriotism and their tutorial rhetoric are each undercut by Swift's chorus of ridicule and deflation. In each case Swift gives his narrators enough rope to hang themselves; their minds and imaginations eventually entangle themselves in a web of words and theories, and common-sense escapes. Gulliver's clear moral vision of a corrupt humanity necessitates his alienation from the world we all live in. With Swift in mind, John Henry Newman described in his *Grammar of Assent* (1870) how 'We judge for ourselves, by our own lights, and on our own principles; and our criterion of truth is not so much the manipulation of propositions, as the intellectual and moral character of the person maintaining them, and the ultimate silent effect of his arguments or conclusions upon our minds.' Like Swift, Newman was concerned to show that we can believe without understanding and that we can also believe what we cannot absolutely prove. Both Gulliver and the Modest Proposer put all their energy into proving, by empirical experience and statistical logic, that action should be based on reason. Swift knew better, and his reductive, deflationary and anarchic wit celebrates the doomed attempts we make to replace the confusion of life with an elegant model which only exists in the restless mind of man. Swift's comic wit graciously invites the reader to believe all he is told, and then demonstrates his credulity when the affable smile turns into a dry mock. His satire, in his own words, 'points at no Defect, / But what all *Mortals* may correct'. There is, accordingly, no escape from the world we have created: this is at once the tragic and the farcical character of existence. Gulliver's final humiliation is to realize that even when his readers are told the unvarnished truth, nobody can recognize it.

Select Bibliography

Biographies

EHRENPREIS, IRVIN. *Swift: The Man, his Works, and the Age*, 3 volumes, London, 1962–83; the definitive biography.

EHRENPREIS, IRVIN. *The Personality of Swift*, London and Cambridge, Mass., 1958.

QUINTANA, RICARDO. *The Mind and Art of Jonathan Swift*, 1936; revised edition, London and New York, 1953; a useful general introduction.

Editions

See 'Note on Text' above, p. 10. For *A Tale of a Tub*, see Angus Ross and David Woolley (eds.), *'A Tale of a Tub' and Other Works*, Oxford, 1986.

Background

BECKETT, J. C. *The Making of Modern Ireland 1603–1923*, 1966; revised edition, London, 1981.

DOWNIE, A. J. *Robert Harley and the Press: Propaganda and Public Opinion in the Age of Swift and Defoe*, Cambridge, 1979.

FERGUSON, O. W. *Jonathan Swift and Ireland*, Urbana, 1962.

HARTH, PHILLIP. *Swift and Anglican Rationalism: The Religious Background of 'A Tale of a Tub'*, Chicago, 1961.

JONES, R. F. *Ancients and Moderns: A Study of the Rise of the Scientific Movement in Seventeenth-Century England*, second edition, St Louis, 1961.

LANDA, LOUIS. *Swift and the Church of Ireland*, Oxford, 1954.

PROBYN, CLIVE T. *Jonathan Swift: The Contemporary Background*, Manchester and New York, 1978: twenty-three extracts from Swift's period illustrating his themes and ideas, including Petty, Molyneux's *Case of Ireland*, Locke, etc.

On Gulliver's Travels

ADAMS, PERCY G. *Travelers and Travel-Liars, 1660–1800*, Berkeley, 1978.

ADAMS, PERCY G. *Travel Literature and the Evolution of the Novel*, Lexington, 1983.

CARNOCHAN, W. B. *Lemuel Gulliver's Mirror for Man*, Berkeley, 1968.

CASE, A. E. *Four Essays on 'Gulliver's Travels'*, Princeton, 1945.

CRANE, R. S. 'The Houyhnhnms, the Yahoos, and the History of Ideas', in *Reason and Imagination*, ed. J. A. Mazzeo, New York and London, 1962, pp. 231–53.

EDDY, W. A. *'Gulliver's Travels': A Critical Study*, Princeton and London, 1923, reprinted Gloucester, Mass., 1963 (actually on the sources).

FOSTER, MILTON P. (ed.) *A Casebook on Gulliver among the Houyhnhnms*, New York, 1961.

FRYE, ROLAND M. 'Swift's Yahoos and the Christian Symbols for Sin', *Journal of the History of Ideas*, XV (1954), 201–17.

LOCK, F. P. *The Politics of 'Gulliver's Travels'*, Oxford, 1980.

RAWSON, CLAUDE. *Gulliver and the Gentle Reader: Studies in Swift and Our Time*, London, 1973.

ROSENHEIM, EDWARD J. 'Swift and the Atterbury Case', in *The Augustan Milieu*, ed. H. K. Miller and others, Oxford, 1971, pp. 174–204.

General

BROWN, NORMAN O. *Life Against Death: The Psychoanalytical Meaning of History*, New York, 1959; chapter entitled 'The Excremental Vision', pp. 179–201.

BULLITT, JOHN M. *Jonathan Swift and the Anatomy of Satire: A Study of Satiric Technique*, Cambridge, Mass., 1953.

EWALD, W. B. *The Masks of Jonathan Swift*, Oxford, 1954.

PAULSON, RONALD F. *Theme and Structure in Swift's 'Tale of a Tub'*, New Haven, 1960.

PRICE, MARTIN. *Swift's Rhetorical Art: A Study in Structure and Meaning*, New Haven, 1953.

PROBYN, CLIVE T. (ed.) *The Art of Jonathan Swift*, London, 1978; a collection of critical essays.

ROSENHEIM, EDWARD J. *Swift and the Satirist's Art*, Chicago, 1963.

STARKMAN, MIRIAM J.   *Swift's Satire on Learning in 'A Tale of a Tub'*, Princetown, 1950.
WILLIAMS, KATHLEEN (ed.)   *Swift: The Critical Heritage*, London, 1970; Swift's critical reception from 1704 to 1819.

Chronology of Anglo-Irish History 1603–1782

1603–9   English common law enforced throughout Ireland
1608–10   Settlement of the Ulster plantation
1641   Beginning of Ulster rising (23 October)
1642   Civil war breaks out in England (August)
1649   Execution of Charles I (30 January)
1649–50   Cromwell's campaigns in Ireland
1652–3   Cromwellian land confiscation
1658   Death of Cromwell (3 September)
1660   Restoration of Charles II
          Foundation of Royal Society (chartered in 1662)
          Act of Settlement
          Navigation Act, restricting Irish trade (as in 1663 and 1671)
1661   Charles II's Irish parliament
1662–9   James Butler, Ist Duke of Ormond, Lord Lieutenant of
          Ireland (as in 1667–85)
1663–6   Legislation restricting export of Irish cattle to England (a
          'public and common nuisance'); Woollen and Navigation
          Acts of the same nature and purpose
1668   Sir William Temple negotiates the Triple Alliance (England,
          Holland and Sweden) against France
1678–81   'Popish Plot': Exclusion Crisis of 1679–81, attempts to ex-
          clude James, Catholic brother of Charles II, from suc-
          cession; London trial and execution for treason of Oliver
          Plunket, Roman Catholic Archbishop of Armagh (July
          1681)
1683   Foundation of Dublin Philosophical Society (Sir William
          Petty as president; members included William King, Nar-
          cissus Marsh, and William Molyneux, secretary)
1685   Death of Charles II (February) and accession of James II
1687   Richard Talbot, Earl of Tyrconnel, appointed Lord Deputy;
          head of Irish army; embarks on policy of Catholic appoint-
          ments in the army, judiciary, corporations, and university;
          James issues Declaration of Indulgence, suspending tests
          and granting liberty of worship to Protestants and Catholics;
          exodus of Protestants begins

1688–9   Attainder Act: James provides for largely Catholic resettlement of Ireland
Revolution in England
James arrives in Ireland (12 March)
Siege of Derry (19 April to 28 July)
James's Irish parliament (May–July), almost entirely Catholic (the 'Patriot Parliament')
William King, Dean of St Patrick's, imprisoned by Jacobite government

1690   William III arrives in Ireland (June); defeats the army of James at the Battle of the Boyne (1 July); James flees to France

1691   Treaty of Limerick (3 October): provisions for toleration of Catholic worship (not ratified by Irish parliament) and Catholic share of land reduced to about one seventh. Act of 1691 asserts Protestant monopoly of Irish parliament

1691–1703   Williamite land confiscations

1692   Catholics excluded from Irish parliament

1695   Beginning of penal legislation against Catholics

1698   English House of Commons rejects Ireland's claim for independence under the crown, rejecting William Molyneux's *The Case of Ireland being bound by acts of parliament in England stated* as 'bold and pernicious assertions'

1699   Act to restrict the export of Irish woollens

1701   Act of Settlement fixed Protestant succession in the House of Hanover
Corporation of Dublin erects equestrian statue of William III, 'the deliverer', on College Green; the focal point for Irish Protestant celebrations each 4 November

1702   William III dies (March); accession of Queen Anne

1704   Sacramental Test Act extended to Ireland

1707   Act of Union with Scotland; Swift writes *Story of an Injured Lady* (i.e. Ireland)

1707–9   Swift represents Irish clergy seeking remission of ecclesiastical taxes, in London

1709–10   Sacheverell affair
Fall of the Whigs; Tory victory (ministry of Harley and St John)

1711   Occasional Conformity Bill prevents dissenters taking occasional Anglican communion in order to qualify for public office

1713	Swift installed Dean of St Patrick's Cathedral, Dublin (June)
	Peace treaties between England and France concluded at Utrecht, ending War of Spanish Succession; France abandons Pretender and recognizes House of Hanover
1714	Death of Queen Anne; Elector of Hanover proclaimed George I
1715	Jacobite rising in Scotland
1719	Declaratory Act enforces dependence of Ireland, denying Irish Lords power to alter judgements made in England
	Toleration Acts extended to Irish Protestants (Test Acts thereafter modified until their abolition in 1780)
1720	English parliament abolishes right of the Irish House of Lords to act as Court of Appeal (March); Swift publishes *A Proposal for the Universal Use of Irish Manufacture; ... utterly rejecting and renouncing everything wearable that comes from England*
1722	Patent for William Wood's copper coinage (*July*)
1724	Hugh Boulter, Bishop of Bristol, appointed Archbishop of Armagh: the principal agent of England's Irish policy (November)
	The Drapier's Letters (February onwards)
1727	Death of George I (June); succeeded by son, George II
1730	Swift given Freedom of the City of Dublin
1731	Establishment of the Dublin Society for 'the improvement of agriculture and other useful arts'
1739	Declaration of war against Spain
1740–1	Famine in Ireland
1741	Motions in parliament to remove Walpole; resigns in 1742
1741–2	Handel visits Dublin; in April 1742 *Messiah* first performed in the Music Hall, Fishamble Street
1745	Lord Chesterfield appointed Lord Lieutenant of Ireland
	Jacobite rising in Scotland
1759	Restrictions against importation of Irish cattle into England removed; villages destroyed to extend pasture
1782	Sacramental Test Act abolished
	Irish parliamentary independence conceded by English parliament

FOR THE BEST IN PAPERBACKS, LOOK FOR THE

In every corner of the world, on every subject under the sun, Penguin represents quality and variety – the very best in publishing today.

For complete information about books available from Penguin – including Pelicans, Puffins, Peregrines and Penguin Classics – and how to order them, write to us at the appropriate address below. Please note that for copyright reasons the selection of books varies from country to country.

In the United Kingdom: Please write to *Dept E.P., Penguin Books Ltd, Harmondsworth, Middlesex, UB7 0DA*

In the United States: Please write to *Dept BA, Penguin, 299 Murray Hill Parkway, East Rutherford, New Jersey 07073*

In Canada: Please write to *Penguin Books Canada Ltd, 2801 John Street, Markham, Ontario L3R 1B4*

In Australia: Please write to the *Marketing Department, Penguin Books Australia Ltd, P.O. Box 257, Ringwood, Victoria 3134*

In New Zealand: Please write to the *Marketing Department, Penguin Books (NZ) Ltd, Private Bag, Takapuna, Auckland 9*

In India: Please write to *Penguin Overseas Ltd, 706 Eros Apartments, 56 Nehru Place, New Delhi, 110019*

In Holland: Please write to *Penguin Books Nederland B.V., Postbus 195, NL–1380AD Weesp, Netherlands*

In Germany: Please write to *Penguin Books Ltd, Friedrichstrasse 10–12, D–6000 Frankfurt Main 1, Federal Republic of Germany*

In Spain: Please write to *Longman Penguin España, Calle San Nicolas 15, E–28013 Madrid, Spain*

In France: Please write to *Penguin Books Ltd, 39 Rue de Montmorency, F-75003, Paris, France*

In Japan: Please write to *Longman Penguin Japan Co Ltd, Yamaguchi Building, 2–12–9 Kanda Jimbocho, Chiyoda-Ku, Tokyo 101, Japan*

PENGUIN REFERENCE BOOKS

The Penguin Guide to the Law

This acclaimed reference book is designed for everyday use and forms the most comprehensive handbook ever published on the law as it affects the individual.

The Penguin Medical Encyclopedia

Covers the body and mind in sickness and in health, including drugs, surgery, history, institutions, medical vocabulary and many other aspects. 'Highly commendable' – *Journal of the Institute of Health Education*

The Penguin French Dictionary

This invaluable French–English, English–French dictionary includes both the literary and dated vocabulary needed by students, and the up-to-date slang and specialized vocabulary (scientific, legal, sporting, etc) needed in everyday life. As a passport to the French language it is second to none.

A Dictionary of Literary Terms

Defines over 2,000 literary terms (including lesser known, foreign language and technical terms) explained with illustrations from literature past and present.

The Penguin Dictionary of Troublesome Words

A witty, straightforward guide to the pitfalls and hotly disputed issues in standard written English, illustrated with examples and including a glossary of grammatical terms and an appendix on punctuation.

The Concise Cambridge Italian Dictionary

Compiled by Barbara Reynolds, this work is notable for the range of examples provided to illustrate the exact meaning of Italian words and phrases. It also contains a pronunciation guide and a reference grammar.

THE LIBRARY OF EVERY CIVILIZED PERSON

John Aubrey	**Brief Lives**
Francis Bacon	**The Essays**
James Boswell	**The Life of Johnson**
Sir Thomas Browne	**The Major Works**
John Bunyan	**The Pilgrim's Progress**
Edmund Burke	**Reflections on the Revolution in France**
Thomas de Quincey	**Confessions of an English Opium Eater**
	Recollections of the Lakes and the Lake Poets
Daniel Defoe	**A Journal of the Plague Year**
	Moll Flanders
	Robinson Crusoe
	Roxana
	A Tour Through the Whole Island of Great Britain
Henry Fielding	**Jonathan Wild**
	Joseph Andrews
	The History of Tom Jones
Oliver Goldsmith	**The Vicar of Wakefield**
William Hazlitt	**Selected Writings**
Thomas Hobbes	**Leviathan**
Samuel Johnson/	**A Journey to the Western Islands of**
James Boswell	**Scotland/The Journal of a Tour to the Hebrides**
Charles Lamb	**Selected Prose**
Samuel Richardson	**Clarissa**
	Pamela
Adam Smith	**The Wealth of Nations**
Tobias Smollet	**Humphry Clinker**
Richard Steele and Joseph Addison	Selections from the **Tatler** and the **Spectator**
Laurence Sterne	**The Life and Opinions of Tristram Shandy, Gentleman**
	A Sentimental Journey Through France and Italy
Jonathan Swift	**Gulliver's Travels**
Dorothy and William Wordsworth	**Home at Grasmere**

THE LIBRARY OF EVERY CIVILIZED PERSON

Matthew Arnold	**Selected Prose**
Jane Austen	**Emma**
	Lady Susan, The Watsons, Sanditon
	Mansfield Park
	Northanger Abbey
	Persuasion
	Pride and Prejudice
	Sense and Sensibility
Anne Brontë	**The Tenant of Wildfell Hall**
Charlotte Brontë	**Jane Eyre**
	Shirley
	Villette
Emily Brontë	**Wuthering Heights**
Samuel Butler	**Erewhon**
	The Way of All Flesh
Thomas Carlyle	**Selected Writings**
Wilkie Collins	**The Moonstone**
	The Woman in White
Charles Darwin	**The Origin of the Species**
Charles Dickens	**American Notes for General Circulation**
	Barnaby Rudge
	Bleak House
	The Christmas Books
	David Copperfield
	Dombey and Son
	Great Expectations
	Hard Times
	Little Dorrit
	Martin Chuzzlewit
	The Mystery of Edwin Drood
	Nicholas Nickleby
	The Old Curiosity Shop
	Oliver Twist
	Our Mutual Friend
	The Pickwick Papers
	Selected Short Fiction
	A Tale of Two Cities

THE LIBRARY OF EVERY CIVILIZED PERSON

Benjamin Disraeli	Sybil
George Eliot	Adam Bede
	Daniel Deronda
	Felix Holt
	Middlemarch
	The Mill on the Floss
	Romola
	Scenes of Clerical Life
	Silas Marner
Elizabeth Gaskell	Cranford and Cousin Phillis
	The Life of Charlotte Brontë
	Mary Barton
	North and South
	Wives and Daughters
Edward Gibbon	The Decline and Fall of the Roman Empire
George Gissing	New Grub Street
Edmund Gosse	Father and Son
Richard Jefferies	Landscape with Figures
Thomas Macaulay	The History of England
Henry Mayhew	Selections from London Labour and The London Poor
John Stuart Mill	On Liberty
William Morris	News from Nowhere and Selected Writings and Designs
Walter Pater	Marius the Epicurean
John Ruskin	'Unto This Last' and Other Writings
Sir Walter Scott	Ivanhoe
Robert Louis Stevenson	Dr Jekyll and Mr Hyde
William Makepeace Thackeray	The History of Henry Esmond
	Vanity Fair
Anthony Trollope	Barchester Towers
	Framley Parsonage
	Phineas Finn
	The Warden
Mrs Humphrey Ward	Helbeck of Bannisdale
Mary Wollstonecraft	Vindication of the Rights of Women

THE LIBRARY OF EVERY CIVILIZED PERSON

Netochka Nezvanova   Fyodor Dostoyevsky

Dostoyevsky's first book tells the story of 'Nameless Nobody' and introduces many of the themes and issues which will dominate his great masterpieces.

Selections from the Carmina Burana   A verse translation by David Parlett

The famous songs from the *Carmina Burana* (made into an oratorio by Carl Orff) tell of lecherous monks and corrupt clerics, drinkers and gamblers, and the fleeting pleasures of youth.

Fear and Trembling   Søren Kierkegaard

A profound meditation on the nature of faith and submission to God's will which examines with startling originality the story of Abraham and Isaac.

Selected Prose   Charles Lamb

Lamb's famous essays (under the strange pseudonym of Elia) on anything and everything have long been celebrated for their apparently innocent charm; this major new edition allows readers to discover the darker and more interesting aspects of Lamb.

The Picture of Dorian Gray   Oscar Wilde

Wilde's superb and macabre novella, one of his supreme works, is reprinted here with a masterly Introduction and valuable Notes by Peter Ackroyd.

A Treatise of Human Nature   David Hume

A universally acknowledged masterpiece by 'the greatest of all British Philosophers' – A. J. Ayer

THE LIBRARY OF EVERY CIVILIZED PERSON

A Passage to India   E. M. Forster

Centred on the unresolved mystery in the Marabar Caves, Forster's great work provides the definitive evocation of the British Raj.

The Republic   Plato

The best-known of Plato's dialogues, *The Republic* is also one of the supreme masterpieces of Western philosophy whose influence cannot be overestimated.

The Life of Johnson   James Boswell

Perhaps the finest 'life' ever written, Boswell's *Johnson* captures for all time one of the most colourful and talented figures in English literary history.

Remembrance of Things Past (3 volumes)   Marcel Proust

This revised version by Terence Kilmartin of C. K. Scott Moncrieff's original translation has been universally acclaimed – available for the first time in paperback.

Metamorphoses   Ovid

A golden treasury of myths and legends which has proved a major influence on Western literature.

A Nietzsche Reader   Friedrich Nietzsche

A superb selection from all the major works of one of the greatest thinkers and writers in world literature, translated into clear, modern English.

The Age of Reason   Jean-Paul Sartre

The first part of Sartre's classic trilogy, set in the volatile Paris summer of 1938, is itself 'a dynamic, deeply disturbing novel' (Elizabeth Bowen) which tackles some of the major issues of our time.

Three Lives   Gertrude Stein

A turning point in American literature, these portraits of three women – thin, worn Anna, patient, gentle Lena and the complicated, intelligent Melanctha – represented in 1909 one of the pioneering examples of modernist writing.

Doctor Faustus   Thomas Mann

Perhaps the most convincing description of an artistic genius ever written, this portrait of the composer Leverkuhn is a classic statement of one of Mann's obsessive themes: the discord between genius and sanity.

The New Machiavelli   H. G. Wells

This autobiography of a man who has thrown up a glittering political career and marriage to go into exile with the woman he loves also contains an illuminating Introduction by Melvyn Bragg.

The Collected Poems of Stevie Smith

Amused, amusing and deliciously barbed, this volume includes many poems which dwell on death; as a whole, though, as this first complete edition in paperback makes clear, Smith's poetry affirms an irrepressible love of life.

Rhinoceros / The Chairs / The Lesson   Eugène Ionesco

Three great plays by the man who was one of the founders of what has come to be known as the Theatre of the Absurd.

The Second Sex   Simone de Beauvoir

This great study of Woman is a landmark in feminist history, drawing together insights from biology, history and sociology as well as literature, psychoanalysis and mythology to produce one of the supreme classics of the twentieth century.

The Bridge of San Luis Rey   Thornton Wilder

On 20 July 1714 the finest bridge in all Peru collapsed, killing 5 people. Why? Did it reveal a latent pattern in human life? In this beautiful, vivid and compassionate investigation, Wilder asks some searching questions in telling the story of the survivors.

Parents and Children   Ivy Compton-Burnett

This richly entertaining introduction to the world of a unique novelist brings to light the deadly claustrophobia within a late-Victorian upper-middle-class family . . .

Vienna 1900   Arthur Schnitzler

These deceptively languid sketches, four 'games with love and death', lay bare an astonishing and disturbing world of sexual turmoil (which anticipates Freud's discoveries) beneath the smooth surface of manners and convention.

Confessions of Zeno   Italo Svevo

Zeno, an innocent in a corrupt world, triumphs in the end through his stoic acceptance of his own failings in this extraordinary, experimental novel which fuses memory, obsession and desire.

The House of Mirth   Edith Wharton

Lily Bart – beautiful, intelligent and charming – is trapped like a butterfly in the inverted jam jar of wealthy New York society . . . This tragic comedy of manners was one of Wharton's most shocking and innovative books.

FOR THE BEST IN PAPERBACKS, LOOK FOR THE

PENGUIN MODERN CLASSICS

The Glass Bead Game   Hermann Hesse

In a perfect world where passions are tamed by meditation, where academic discipline and order are paramount, scholars, isolated from hunger, family, children and women, play the ultra-aesthetic glass bead game. This is Hesse's great novel, which has made a significant contribution to contemporary philosophic literature.

If It Die   André Gide

A masterpiece of French prose, *If It Die* is Gide's record of his childhood, his friendships, his travels, his sexual awakening and, above all, the search for truth which characterizes his whole life and all his writing.

Dark as the Grave wherein my Friend is Laid   Malcolm Lowry

A Dantean descent into hell, into the infernal landscape of Mexico, the same Mexico as Lowry's *Under the Volcano*, a country of mental terrors and spiritual chasms.

The Collected Short Stories   Katherine Mansfield

'She could discern in a trivial event or an insignificant person some moving revelation or motive or destiny . . . There is an abundance of that tender and delicate art which penetrates the appearances of life to discover the elusive causes of happiness and grief' – W. E. Williams in his Introduction to *The Garden Party and Other Stories*

Sanctuary   William Faulkner

Faulkner draws America's Deep South exactly as he saw it: seething with life and corruption; and *Sanctuary* asserts itself as a compulsive and unsparing vision of human nature.

The Expelled and Other Novellas   Samuel Beckett

Rich in verbal and situational humour, the four stories in this volume offer the reader a fascinating insight into Beckett's preoccupation with the helpless individual consciousness, a preoccupation which has remained constant throughout Beckett's work.

FOR THE BEST IN PAPERBACKS, LOOK FOR THE 🐧

PENGUIN MASTERSTUDIES

This comprehensive list, designed for advanced level and first-year under-graduate studies, includes:

SUBJECTS
Applied Mathematics
Biology
Drama: Text into Performance
Geography
Pure Mathematics

LITERATURE
Absalom and Achitophel
Barchester Towers
Dr Faustus
Eugenie Grandet
Gulliver's Travels
Joseph Andrews
The Mill on the Floss
A Passage to India
Persuasion *and* Emma
Portrait of a Lady
Tender in the Night
Vanity Fair

CHAUCER
The Knight's Tale
The Pardoner's Tale
The Prologue to the Canterbury Tales
A Chaucer Handbook

SHAKESPEARE
Hamlet
Measure for Measure
Much Ado About Nothing
A Shakespeare Handbook